Reiser's Ramblings
By Father Bernard Reiser

First Edition

Additional copies of the book can be ordered online at www.ReiserRelief.org.

Front cover portrait of Father Bernard Reiser by: Mark Sanislo
www.MarkSanislo.com

Reiser's Ramblings edited by: Jacqueline Nasseff Hilgert

Book and jacket design by:
Traditions Communications LLC
17272 - 605th Avenue
Janesville, MN 56048
www.TraditionsCommunications.com

Printed in the United States of America

International Book Standard Number
ISBN: 978-0-615-36478-0

Library of Congress Control Number: 2010904474

Reiser's Ramblings

FR. BERNARD REISER

For Aloys and Ottilia Reiser

They were my strength.
I would not have accomplished anything without them.

Introduction
and Acknowledgments

It typically was late each Sunday before I'd have an opportunity to set down on paper my thoughts for the columns that would become the weekly *Reiser's Rambling*. Often, it was midnight and the only sound in the rectory was the hum coming from the refrigerator. I would sit at the kitchen table – always with a bowl of ice cream because that is my favorite treat – and look at the blank page. Before I'd start I'd offer this quick prayer: "God, what will we write about this week?"

Most weeks, the idea for the weekly column was planted like a seed as I went about my duties visiting the home-bound or those in the hospital, delivering communion, meeting with the scores of dedicated staff or volunteers who we rely upon to keep the parish in tip-top condition and our outreach efforts continuing to make an impact in the world. Sometimes the ideas came while I traveled abroad to experience a new land and foreign culture. Other times, the idea for the weekly Rambling came while taking a simple walk around the grounds or being diverted from my schedule by illness or weather or an offer for lunch with a friend. I often used a dictaphone, as that was a convenient way to get my thoughts across to the secretary who was in charge of typing the column each Monday. Always, though, the columns were polished up at the kitchen table near midnight, helped along by spoonfuls of delicious ice cream and sometimes a cookie or two.

The columns for the weekly bulletin stopped, of course, when I retired as Epiphany's pastor. But many of you have kept them in binders that are so heavy I'd be hard-pressed to lift them off the table. My thought not long ago was to assemble all of the *Reiser's Rambling* columns into a book; this anthology of the very best columns is the fulfillment of that idea. I've added some photos

to help illustrate some of my themes. The columns presented in this volume have been organized by theme and there is an introduction to open each section.

It's important to note that all the profits from the sale of this book are being directed to help the poor of Haiti through Reiser Relief. When you read the columns contained within, some written more than twenty-five years ago, I hope you'll find they inspire you twice – once for the subject matter, and once for the knowledge that your purchase has helped poor children get an education and clean drinking water.

I am awestruck to realize that every week, when I asked God what He wanted to write about in the weekly column, an idea always emerged. I'm further awed that so many of you have been so moved by these columns that you've held onto them for so many years.

I have been, and continue to be, blessed to have numerous individuals looking out for my health and well-being; so many people deserve my gratitude that I can't possibly list their names in the short space available here. You know who you are; please trust that you are remembered in my prayers.

As far as those who have had more direct involvement in the completion of this book, I must first give thanks to Jesus and Mary for their unmeasured blessings, guidance and love.

I am grateful also to my parents, Aloys and Ottilia Reiser, and my siblings; they have been the most creative and influential force in my life.

I want to recognize my late housekeeper, Rae Hauck, who was like a second mother to me for twenty-nine years. I want to also recognize photographer Greg Vilina and artist Mark Sanislo for their contributions.

I am grateful to Michele Flaherty, who encouraged me to publish a book of *Reiser's Rambling* columns; she was of great assistance to me in the effort to get the collection organized.

I want to thank all the people who volunteer their time, talent and love, as together we have moved Reiser Relief Inc. to the splendid position it enjoys in all of its relief efforts. Like Christ, you offer hope to the hopeless.

Finally, to all the parishioners of St. Mary of the Lake in White Bear Lake and Epiphany Church in Coon Rapids with whom I shared the sixty years of my priesthood; their kindness and love shown to me was beyond measurement.

Ad Jesum Per Mariam
(To Jesus through Mary)
Father Bernard Reiser †

Contents

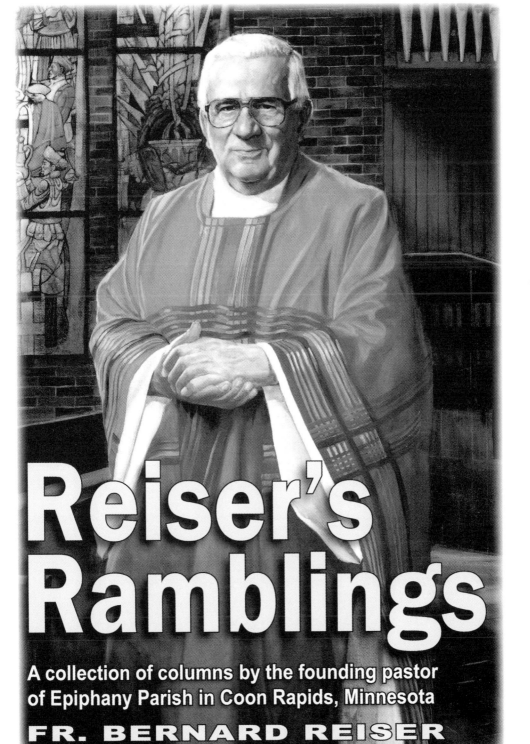

Reiser's Ramblings

A collection of columns by the founding pastor
of Epiphany Parish in Coon Rapids, Minnesota

FR. BERNARD REISER

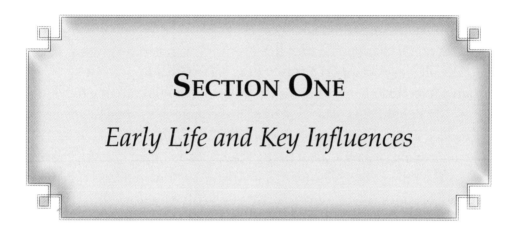

SECTION ONE

Early Life and Key Influences

Early Life and Key Influences

My first memories go back to the farm where my parents, Aloys and Ottilia Reiser, raised me, my brother, and my three sisters during the Great Depression. My father was a truck farmer, meaning the vegetables and meat he raised were trucked into the Minneapolis Farmers Market for sale every day. Farming was a difficult way to support a family during the Great Depression yet my father never faltered in his faith that God would provide for us. My father never said, "We'll try" when telling us something needed to get done. Instead, he told us, "We will!" This lesson in perseverance was one all of his children took to heart.

The little parish we attended in Medina, Minnesota, was called Holy Name, a small country parish of seventy families with a parish school of about eighty students, divided into two classrooms. We attended Holy Name through eighth grade and learned our lessons so well that we outpaced our public school classmates once we moved onto Wayzata High School.

It was at home on our family farm and at events in our small parish where I developed my love for God and the Catholic faith. My parents worked hard, fed us well, loved us and loved each other. Never once did I hear my parents quarrel.

I was ordained in 1949 and have devoted the remainder of my life to the faith, serving God's people, ministering, presiding over baptisms, marriages and funerals, lifting up the needy, helping the poor.

Since my ordination, I have traveled around the globe, witnessed dramatic world events, built up God's church to the best of

My parents, Ottilia and Aloys Reiser.

my ability, and paused once a week to jot down my thoughts on it all. In this first section, I share some of my columns to give you an idea about the early influences that shaped me. †

Sunday was the day
for worship, rest and family

Sundays during my childhood were always a magnificent and wonderful day of the week. It was worth looking forward to because it was a day filled with many delights. You need remember this is over sixty years ago down on the farm. After the morning milking was done, Mass was next on the agenda. It was always a special time of the week and we all had to put on our best clothes. They might not have been stylish, but they were always clean and well pressed. Shirt and tie were an absolute, and everyone had one good shirt that was reserved for Sunday Mass. Mother always said, "The Lord needed to get our very best."

Holy Name Church was a small country parish of only seventy families, and everyone knew everybody else, as well as everybody else's business. Every family had their own particular pew and that's where you took occupancy at every church service. You always knew who was at Sunday Mass, and if they were missing, there was always a cause for alarm, because everyone went. If Uncle Johnny or Aunt Clara were missing, there would be a phone call right after Mass to discover whether or not something had gone wrong; were they sick or had they experienced some tragedy? It wasn't a case of being snoopy, but just being sensitive to any possibility that there was a problem because everybody went to church.

Mass was in Latin except the sermon (they didn't call them "homilies" in those days). We all had our Sunday Missals and followed along very easily. There was always perfect order in Church because Mother was at one end of the pew and Dad on the other end, with the kids in between, and if you had even an ounce of sense, you knew it was imperative that you minded your Ps and Qs. After Mass, the parking lot didn't clear very quickly, because it was a wonderful opportunity for neighbors to pause and visit. The men gathered in one area, the ladies in another, and the kids just ran around, goofing off. The church was not only a place for prayer and worship, but also for socializing, renewing of friendships and keeping up to date on what was happening with the neighbors.

The priest was in charge of all things pertaining to the parish. He was the last word in all matters, and questioning any of his decisions was like challenging the Pope. There weren't a dozen different boards and numerous committee meetings. Times have certainly changed.

The Sunday dinner was always a delightful experience, and for us, chicken was the favorite of the whole family. Mashed potatoes, magnificent gravy, wonderful vegetables and chicken that would certainly have challenged Kentucky Fried were on the Sunday menu. Apple pie reigned supreme, with some of the seasonal varieties such as cherry and pumpkin coming in here and there during the course of the year. Another magnificent dimension of Sunday was freezing a gallon of ice cream. The freezer was an old hand-crank model that required a lot of arm muscle, chipped ice and salt. It was there that I gained a marvelous taste for that delicacy called ice cream, and the years have not diminished my appetite for it.

There was no work on Sunday, except the barn chores, because we felt the Lord wouldn't look too kindly upon it. Farmers are certainly dependent on God for good weather, with a good balance of sun and rain, early springs and late frosts. God was certainly in charge, so we didn't feel we should challenge His rules and wishes.

Entertainment was homemade and always occupied a good part of Sunday afternoon and evening. The season of the year determined the activities. Winter was filled with tobogganing, skiing, skating and playing wonderful games inside the house, along with an ample supply of popcorn, homemade beer and delicious fudge. Summer season offered grand opportunities for fishing in the local lakes and playing softball at the parish ball field. On special Sundays, we sat along the shore of Lake Minnetonka and watched the motor-boat races; this was the ultimate in excitement, adventure and entertainment.

Mother and Dad came from large families, so there were always a lot of visitors on Sundays. People just dropped in, invitations weren't considered necessary. Each parish had their own Sunday festival during the summer or fall, so that was always a must for the family to attend. There would be a dinner and a wide variety of games and entertainment.

They were wonderful days, because everything centered around the family; we prayed together, worked together, ate together and played together. You not only loved your family members, but they were friends. ✝

The Reiser family, pictured in 1949. Seated, from left, are: Sister Bertrand O.S.B., Aloys, Ottilia and Fr. Bernard Reiser. Standing, from left, are: Lynn Maciej, Alex Reiser and Rosemary Leger.

Relationships are a cherished dimension of human experience

The mild winter we are having this year reminds me of over sixty years ago when our winters were often extremely severe. I remember one entire month in which the temperature never rose above zero degrees and much of that month was between ten degrees and twenty degrees below.

The snowstorms seemed far more severe because there wasn't the modern snow removal equipment, with big trucks and snow blowers to get the snow off the roads quickly. Oftentimes the country roads were snowbound for nearly a week until the V-shaped horse-drawn plows were able to make it to your area. There would be six teams of horses on the wooden plow with the steel edges on the sides. Every crew had a good number of men with shovels to break open the drifts and the deep areas of snow. It was always exciting to see this great crew come slowly down the road, for it meant getting back to civilization once again.

Our township road came as far as our property line and from there to the house was our responsibility to open. That portion of the road had a rather sizable hill that led down to the farm yard and so we were always extremely grateful when the crew decided to do that portion of the road, which was a good quarter of a mile.

One favor certainly deserved another, so when they came to our yard, the men would tie up the horses and come into the house to be warmed up a bit. Mother always had dozens of home-made raised donuts on hand and a good supply of homemade wine to warm their innards. There weren't any coffee breaks out on the road so the men and horses deserved a bit of rest. With caps and heavy coats thrown on the floor, they sat around and played a few games of cards while enjoying ample donuts and wine. Some of the men on the crew were town board members so there was no fear of higher authority reprimanding these hard working men for a little breather on their day's work experience. With a few good glasses of grape wine and half a dozen raised donuts inside, the men were ready to attack some more town roads loaded with snow.

Country life then had a wonderful spirit of neighborliness and of helping one another. Fellowship and friendship filled the human cup to overflowing and everybody knew everybody else. When someone was sick, there was no need to put out a call for help because the neighbors were right there to give a helping hand. When there was a need, they didn't call and say, "Let me know if there is something I can do." They just did it. The hot dishes and the cakes just appeared at your door and helping hands were there summer or winter to ease the burden of a stressed neighbor.

Our computerized society has certainly moved things at lightning speed and jobs are performed at swiftness beyond expression. People become rather independent and oftentimes live in their own little world, oblivious of neighbor and friend down the street. All of our advancement and technology often puts aside the great human relationships that should exist between neighbor, relative and friend, and those are realities of life that are irreplaceable, and certainly a cherished dimension of human experience. We have advanced in many areas but we have lost ground in others.

Oh yes, I forgot to mention, that we kids often prayed for good snowstorms, and the more severe the better. It meant no school and wonderful opportunities for house games, popcorn, fudge, sledding, skating and all of the other wonderful winter experiences. Yes, there were advantages to not having snow-blowers or heavy mechanized equipment to move the snow real quickly. †

Homespun-care cured all our ills

I turned on the faucet and filled my glass with a nice, fresh drink of water. What a wonderful convenience that we so take for granted. My memories took me back to those early days on the farm, sixty-five years ago. There was a bucket of water with a dipper in it on the kitchen cupboard and that was the drinking supply for everyone in the household, including visitors. Just slip the dipper into the bucket of water and pull out some clear H_2O that most of the time was not very cold, or anywhere near it, but it was wet and satisfied the thirst. It never occurred to us that we could be passing on any contagious disease, one to the other. I guess the common dipper, a germ carrier, acted as a vaccination against the ordinary ills and sickness of daily life. It must have worked wonders, because none of us ever went to the doctor except my brother Alex who had an appendectomy when he was in his early teens.

I need to tell you how the water got into that bucket. We had a hand pump a few yards from the kitchen door that took lots of muscle on occasion to bring the water up to the proper level. When the wind was blowing strong and the temperatures were far below zero, it was a bit of a challenge to stand out there and pump the water by hand. One feared it would freeze before you got the liquid into the kitchen. Obviously there was no running water in the house; it was entirely a hand engineered project.

We must have built up a lot of immunities or something, because it seems we were always healthy; but of course, there was always that extra little tonic coming with the first traces of cold weather in the fall, namely a tablespoon of cod liver oil every day. God knows no virus would have a chance against that cod liver oil. The reward for the cod liver oil was a quarter piece of orange for each who lined up to take their daily dose. I was thinking I should start taking cod liver oil again. It surely did the trick in those days and might be an extra shot in the arm for me during these later years in life.

There were lots of home remedies that Mother pulled out of her bag of cures that seemed to work in a marvelous fashion. Any sign of a cold would bring on the usual therapy, some good strong red ointment, that virtually burned the skin right off of your chest, was put on in good measure, mixed with a bit of goose grease to ease the sting. I often believed that it penetrated right through to my backbone the way it seemed to edge its way through like a sharp-edged dagger. Your chest was wrapped with wool and flannel material that made your chest feel like some red hot oven. No virus stood a chance against that unrelenting attack by the red ointment. It was like the Marines or the commandoes hitting the beaches of the South Pacific with persistent force during the Second World War. The bottom line was that it worked, and after all, that's what really counts.

We didn't see many cough drops around, for Mama had her own remedy for a cough, namely, lots of honey in a quart jar along with a few squeezed lemons, two or three shots of good brandy and then boiling water to mix it all up in great style. You were tucked into bed and soon had sugar plums dancing in your head and a very peaceful, sound, and restful night. It was a very tasty remedy and one that certainly justified faking a cough or two to enjoy the remedy, even when not needed.

Open infections were treated with a good hot poultice. For the life of me, I can't remember what it was made out of, but it surely had a very different smell and it drew out the infection and poison about as quickly as a suction pump draining the water out of a flooded basement.

Mother didn't get her medical training at the University of Minnesota or Marquette University, but her mother gave it to her in grand style and so it went back from one generation to the next. No medical diplomas hanging on the kitchen wall, but if it worked, it was great and if it didn't work, we tried something else next time, hoping that there wouldn't be a next time. ⸙

The Reiser family farmhouse near Wayzata, Minnesota.

Recollections spur appreciation
for modern conveniences

Taking a shower these days isn't a very eventful reality. It takes but a few minutes and is a rather simple procedure; get the water to the right temperature, have a good washcloth, a supply of soap and before too many minutes have elapsed, we step out, refreshed, smelling good and ready for another day. Start-to-finish isn't too long a period of time and even quicker, if we have gotten up a bit late and the pressure is on to move quickly.

In the good old days, it wasn't quite so simple, especially during the winter months. The Saturday night bath routine took a bit of juggling, many measures of patience and a good bit of tolerance on the part of all. Arrangements had to be made a few hours before to get enough water hot for seven to have a reasonable amount of warm water. So large kettles lined the old wood stove in the kitchen. The wash tub, used on Mondays to do the laundry, was brought into the kitchen and placed before the wood stove. The oven door was open to add warmth to the room and to act as a heater for the cold shivering bodies that would grace the tub.

When the water had been placed in the tub, the smallest child went first, after all they were presumed to be the less dirty for not having worked in the fields or the barns, although on some occasions that presumption was not entirely valid. Mama scrubbed down the younger ones to make sure that those areas behind the ears and so forth were well attended to, places perhaps that would be otherwise intentionally overlooked. The first one in of course got the cleaner water, but the negative side was, there wasn't as much water as later on, because we needed to save on the hot water and not blow it all on the first bath. With each succeeding person into the tub, the water became a little less clean, but more water was added so there was compensation. The last one in the tub found the water level very high and comfortable but certainly not as pure and clear as a mountain stream.

Did you want more water, or cleaner water? It really wasn't a debatable question because Mother set the order and there was no cutting rank or sneaking in early. After all, there were rules and there was no challenging the decisions made. A razor strap graced the north wall, just to the right of the kitchen door. Its mere presence sent a message loud and clear to all those who frequented the area, that discipline was a part of life. I never recall it ever being removed from the wall for purpose of chastisement, but its presence certainly was a silent warning of what could happen if a child's will became a bit rebellious.

Thank God there was only one weekly bath. I don't know if a family could have endured more than one of those weekly experiences. But after all, everyone got a fresh, clean towel and that was compensation for any of the previous handicaps.

We still had the Romans beat by a long country mile, because some historians say the Romans seldom bathed, they just splashed a lot of perfume over themselves to smell nice and to hide a lack of cleanliness. Mama never even suggested doing the perfume deal in place of the Saturday night bath, thanks be to God.

Summertime was a whole different deal because then we had the outdoor shower. A fifty-gallon water drum on a high platform with the water warmed by the hot summer sun and it provided a quick shower after a day in the fields; it made you feel like a new person. The shower head wasn't much, nor the water very plentiful for all who used the shower, but it was certainly a far better experience than the tub in front of the open stove during the winter.

Old timers certainly recall these memories in your own life and the younger set can appreciate the different style of life we had more than six decades ago. I'm not pushing to go back to it, but it surely makes one appreciate what is at hand. ✝

The Reiser family farm pictured from above.

Farm life provided many wonderful memories

I remember the days when there were no freezer cabinets in every home and preserving the harvest for the winter months was a bit of a challenge. One alternative was canning, namely putting the food into Mason jars. Canning was always a great undertaking in late summer and fall, when hundreds and hundreds of jars were filled with the wonderful produce of the summer. It was a tedious and long job, but the benefits were most satisfying when you came to eat the food during the cold months of winter.

The cellar was a sight to behold, as you saw shelf-upon-shelf of beans, corn, peas, carrots, tomatoes and all the other varieties of vegetables. It provided a grand array of color and made the foods look very tasty, as they always were. Fruits were also canned in great abundance, namely, apricots, peaches, pears, cherries and plums. We always thanked God for the Mason jar, because it was one of the magnificent containers for food.

The cellar was a marvelous place to store fresh carrots, turnips, beets, onions and potatoes in various bins.

Snowstorms provided no great threat in the winter, because the cellar was well-stocked with food and one could hold out for a good long spell.

Digging the vegetables in the fall was a hard job, but a real delight, for you had seen the various plants grow from the early stages of popping out of the earth in the spring to full maturity in the fall.

The nights were crisp and cool and the days were filled with the invigorating smells of fall. It provided a marvelous meaningfulness to life as you walked so close with God in nature. It seemed as though He was always in your back pocket.

Harvesting the melons was always a delightful time because there was always a bit of time to enjoy a fresh ripe melon in the field, truly an eater's delight. The melons were stored in the oats bin, which provided a very marvelous environment for keeping the melons long into the winter, so you could enjoy some splendid eating many months later.

Pumpkins, squash and other items would be stored safely in the driveway of the hay-barn, where there was always ample protection from the cold with hay, straw and corn stalks.

The harvest always gave a grand feeling of satisfaction for the many months of labor, and the assurance that the kitchen table would be laden with nourishing and tasty food during the many months of winter, when the wind blew cold and the snow was piled high.

Farm life provides many wonderful memories and what a delight it is to bask in them. ⊺

The Reiser family farmhouse, viewed from the yard.

A tribute to a family role model

It's Sunday afternoon and I am on my way to my brother's wake. With a dictaphone in my hand, I shall share a few memories of Alex. It is always difficult to lose a family member for they play such a major role in shaping our lives.

Alex and I shared more than seventy-two years together, and thus there are many wonderful memories of the things we shared, the experiences we had, joys and the sorrows that were ours together. We were raised on a farm and so there were numerous things we did in common. In those days, there was a lot of hard work, so we did many, many things together; working in the fields and in the barns as a team. Most meals were together so there was much socializing, conversation and togetherness while eating, that is often not found in the modern home. Alex was seven years my senior, so he was my mentor, advisor and protector. His wise counsel saved me many bumps, misfortunes and heartaches in life.

He was a very religious person and had extremely high moral standards of life, and these he manifested in a very beautiful manner, and as I saw them lived out in his daily life, they seemed to me to be the normal and natural behavior pattern that one should follow. How fortunate I was to have an excellent role model.

He loved music, was an excellent singer, and a member of the Church choir for at least fifty years. Religion and music make great partners, and how beautifully they enrich the human person and lead them down the right paths of life.

He cherished nature and our farmyard was always arrayed with the beautiful colors of a great variety of flowers that got an early start in his two greenhouses, where all year there were beautiful things happening. The yard was exquisitely kept and the rose beds manifested God's beautiful creative touch in nature.

Fall was always an exciting time of year, because Alex was

a great hunter, and when I was a little fellow he took me along through the woods hunting squirrel, through the fields looking for pheasants and along the shores of the lake to shoot a duck or two. There were rabbits as well, scurrying across the countryside, and during the years of the Great Depression, the early and mid-1930s, the bounty of the hunt was well received at the table.

Alex had an extraordinary mechanical skill. He never went to a trade school or spent an hour in any class, but overhauled the cars, did the welding with gas or electric torches, built buildings and beautiful furniture and plumbing and electrical duties were no great challenge to his innate mechanical skill. All seemed to flow as easily from his hands as marbles from a child's little palm. This was no small irritation for me, for I could scarcely fix a mousetrap or build a good milk stool. Thanks be to God, he stayed on the farm, ran the home place and took care of my parents, while I went on to college, because I certainly would not have gotten a passing grade in all those things he did so easily.

He took care of Mother and Dad in their years of illness, and was indeed a Mother Teresa in our household. †

Alex Reiser kept this beautiful rose garden at the family farm.

Lessons on joyful Priesthood
come from Irish pastor, friend

I first met him on June 11, 1949. It was a Saturday morning and only a week before, I had been ordained a priest at the St. Paul Cathedral. It was a bright sunny day and there was warmth in the air and excitement in my heart as I walked the sidewalk leading to the rectory of St. Mary of the Lake, White Bear Lake, Minnesota. A thin-faced Irish priest, Father Nicholas Finn, met me at the door and greeted me with a spirited welcome. Thus began a relationship which lasted thirty-seven years, fifteen of which were spent working side-by-side serving the needs of St. Mary's parish.

Our years together were pleasant and fruitful. They say that a combination of Irish and German parents produce marvelous off-spring. So also, the Irish/German partnership in the rectory resulted in many good happenings over the years.

Father Nicholas Finn

Father Nick, as his friends called him, was a typical Irishman straight from the Irish sod, coming to America in this early twenties. He had countless stories that delighted his listeners, and each of them I heard repeatedly but always with a different twist.

He taught me much in my years as an assistant, and among those treasures, two are most evident and outstanding. He taught me a love for the priesthood, a wonderful gift that God has shared with me for the glory of God and for service to God's people. Secondly, he taught me to wear with pride my black suit and Roman collar, symbols of my dedication to the Lord and of my ministry as a priest.

Tonight, Sunday evening, I led a prayer service for the repose of his soul. It was a festive occasion, the way he would have liked it, and I shared a half dozen of his favorite stories as I reminisced over the past nearly four decades. There were cookies and coffee afterwards and a good Irish spirit in the air.

Tomorrow morning we will lay his body to rest, but his spirit will live in the hearts of many as his soul enjoys the rewards he has so beautifully prepared for in sixty years of priesthood. Father Nick was ninety-five years of age in body, but his vibrancy and love of life was that of an Irishman, singing along the pathways of the Emerald Isle.

It was great knowing you, Father Nick. Be seeing you on the other side. ✝

Fr. Nick Finn (right) poses with Fr. Bernard Reiser, who was given a 1964 Chevrolet in appreciation for his service to St. Mary of the Lake Church. Fr. Reiser served at the White Bear Lake, Minnesota, parish from 1949 to 1964.

AN
IRISH TRIBUTE

God Then made man,
.....
The Italian for Music and Art,
The French for Fine Food,
The German for Intelligence,
The Swedes for Their Beauty,
The Jew for Religion,

And On and On
Until
he Looked at What
he had Created
and Said,
" This Is All Very Fine But
No One Is having Any Fun.
I Guess I'll have to Make Me
An
IRISHMAN "

This Irish Blessing hangs in the hallway outside Fr. Reiser's Coon Rapids apartment. It is a keepsake from one of Father's trips to Ireland, and it recalls his friendship with Fr. Nick Finn.

Devoted housekeeper took on motherly role

October 5, 1969 was an epic and magnificent day in my life. It was on that day that a small, gentle, frail woman graced my doorway. Her words were softly spoken and her manner was unassuming.

How little I knew that day, that for the next twenty-nine years she would be the most important person in my life. Thousands would move in and out of my life in those nearly three decades, but she would be the anchor that would remain steadfast. As the years unfolded, she would become more than a housekeeper; she became, in every respect, a second mother to me. My first mother died when I was twenty-nine, the greatest loss I had ever experienced in my life for she was the summation of all the goodness that I had discovered in humanity. What a powerful influence a mother has on our life; she molds one like the sculptor molds the soft, fresh clay.

Rae's entering into my life was a blessing beyond expression. It was unbelievable how she resembled my own mother. They had so many similar qualities of life that I often thought God had fashioned them from the same mold. Both spoke quietly and there never was any of the boisterousness that can be so annoying in life. They were women of deep and lasting faith, and Our Lord was their constant companion as they journeyed the pathway to the Eternal Kingdom. Devotion to Mary and the Rosary were as much a part of life as eating or sleeping. They became so close to the Mother of Jesus that they mirrored her in their daily lives. You know the old saying, "You can know who a person is by the friends they keep." Mother and Rae had great friends in Jesus and Mary.

Both of them excelled in the kitchen, where they baked so many tasty foods, from raised donuts to delicious pies, extraordinary angel food cake, caramel rolls topped with nuts were a specialty, and there were baked delights all over the kitchen counter. Meats were prepared like a French chef, vegetables graced the table day-by-day and desserts gave the tasty conclusion to every dinner.

Canning vegetables and fruits were done every summer and fall, and the Mason jars were filled with beautiful color varieties of the fruits and vegetables to be served in winter, spring and early summer. Mom and Rae were queens of the kitchen and they excelled in everything they undertook.

Rae Hauck

Washing clothes was done daily and cleaning was on a methodical schedule. Beautiful items were knit and crocheted and hundreds were the beneficiaries of one of those precious and splendid gifts.

As the years unfolded, Rae more and more became my second mother, and the beautiful, thoughtful questions were there: "Do you have your rubbers, and a warm enough coat? Are there enough blankets on your bed?" and the hundred other concerns mothers show for their children.

On October 22, 1998 Rae celebrated her ninety-second birthday. The very next day, October 23, she was born into Eternal Life, where they do not count the years but bask in the beauties, the glories and the joys of God Himself.

Most people are blessed with only one mother; I have been blessed by two. I look forward to sharing Eternity with both. †

Rae Hauck was a devoted housekeeper and mother figure
to Fr. Reiser. She lived to see her 92nd birthday.

This memorial to Fr. Reiser's parents, Aloys and Ottilia,
his brother Alex, and longtime housekeeper
Rae Hauck, stands outside the front entrance
of Epiphany Church in Coon Rapids, Minnesota.

SECTION TWO

The Wonder of God's Creation

The Wonder of God's Creation

Spring is always a very exciting time of the year, a time when all nature breaks forth with extraordinary exuberance. The cold loses its grip on the wonders of nature and the melting snow pack transforms into rivulets of water running here, there and everywhere. With the softening earth, pockets of green emerge from the dark graves of once-frozen soil. The early flowers of spring push through the crust with enthusiasm to capture the bright rays of a warm spring sun or to delight in the pleasant showers that typically come in April.

I can remember, as a little boy of six or seven, going with Mother into the woods at springtime to discover the little blue and pink flowers that were the first to add splendor and charm to the floor of the woods as creation began to awaken. Bushes and trees formed little leaf buds that soon unfolded into lush branches of green. The songs of the chattering birds always sounded sweeter in springtime, with the red-breasted robin giving assurance that the long winter had finally passed.

Spring is a time when all creation breaks forth with a new symphony of life. The death of winter is step by step replaced with the explosiveness of new life.

How appropriate it is that Easter comes in springtime. As nature unfolds in the spring, it brings new hope and assurance of the forthcoming wonder of summer and the golden colors of fall. So Easter brings assurance of new life, spiritually. It gives us hope that there is something great and wonderful beyond the suffering, pain and trial of human experience. It gives us assurance that there is something magnificent beyond the tears and sorrows of our earthly life.

Easter brings hope to a world that often appears hopeless. It brings comfort to the sorrows and loses of life. Easter gives the assurance that there is only one disaster and that is the loss of the great reward in the Heavenly kingdom. It gives the assurance that God is a loving God and that even though the trials of life seem unending and multiplied beyond expression, there is something good and glorious to follow.

There are examples of the glory and wonder of the blessing God showers upon us to be found everywhere in nature, no matter the season. Oftentimes, though, the business of life keeps us from noticing the swelling bud, the leafing canopy, the tender blossom.

Every now and then, I used the *Reiser's Rambling* column to encourage my parishioners to slow down and smell the roses, to take note of the wonder that is our planet, our Eden right here on Earth, the blessings shared by a generous God. †

Spring is time to sow new beginnings

Spring is a wonderful time of year. There is such an element of freshness and newness of life. The fresh spring rains wash everything nice and clean; beautiful blades of green grass with a wide range of color and hues appear here, there and everywhere. The tulips with their marvelous delicate blossoms like so many trumpets, proclaiming that nature has come alive once more and the vibrancy and enthusiasm of existence should be enjoyed by all from the very depths of their being. The red-breasted robins are always a beautiful sign of the season, along with the geese making their way back north, and the Mallards searching for a new nesting place near fresh waters. The mornings are refreshingly cool and the evenings are snapping with the unfolding of the buds, with their announcement of new beginnings and new life.

Winter is gone with its cold and snow and piercing cold winds. How quickly we forget and lay aside the woes of a difficult winter as we open our hearts and arms to the newness of spring.

The season of spring gives a wonderful message to each and every one of us on how we need to live out our lives. How we need to set aside the difficulties, the problems, the misunderstandings, perhaps the quarrels and fights of yesterday, putting them away completely, plowing them under so to speak, so that today can be a new start, a new beginning.

How often people hold onto the grudges of yesterday, the misunderstandings, the hurts, the unkindness of word or deed. How good it would be for us to spade under all these things of yesterday and enjoy the fresh springtime of a new day. It's a great way to live life and it's so much more enjoyable and certainly far easier.

Why don't you give it a start tomorrow morning, saying that today is that new day of life, a new chance to live life out as God wishes us to live it, by serving Him and being kind and generous to our fellow humans, a new springtime, every day. ✝

A science book and a crucifix travel well together

With Holy Week upon us in a couple of days, we shall be reflecting on the suffering of Jesus. We will journey with Him from the Garden of Gethsemane and the bloody sweat to the court of Annas, the high priest, then to Caiphas, and then on to Pilate. The terrible scourging follows, then the crowning of thorns, carrying the cross and the crucifixion.

To capture the impact of all of the above, we must reflect continually on who this central figure is, the God who created a universe.

We often lose sight of what this word "Creator" really means. Creator of what? A reflection on the vastness of the universe deepens a person's awareness of who it is that carries the cross and how much He must love us to do what He did.

A Readers Digest book had the following scientific facts under Portrait of the Universe:

Looking at the sun and the stars is like gazing backward down a time tunnel. What is seen from the earth is not the stars as they are, but as they were when the light rays left the various heavenly bodies.

Light travels at 186,000 miles a second and, at this speed, takes eight minutes to reach the earth from the sun. By the same token the closest star to the earth's solar system, Proxima Centauri, is seen not as it is but as it was 4.25 years ago.

With powerful telescopes it is possible to look back millions of years into the past of the universe, and by linking telescopes with sensitive photographic plates, even farther back to a staggering billions of years ago.

With man's ever increasing knowledge and use of more and more sophisticated equipment, we are more aware than ever that the earth is an insignificant dot when measured against the overwhelming backdrop of space.

Only infinite power could fashion such wonders beyond expression. A book of science and a crucifix make great traveling companions. What a great God we have! ✝

The Creator reveals beauty in millions of ways

There were four of them, each fashioned with an exquisiteness that would challenge the most artistic hand and imaginative mind.

The color they shared with admiring eyes was a restful and delightful pink. Their form resembled a heart with white extensions like well-designed spears extended from an opening in the underside. Thread-like hangers of green supported each from a delicate green branch.

I held them to my desk lamp and discovered how perfectly each had been fashioned, each done so excellently well that the Creator deemed it worth repeating.

I'm not a botanist but I guess they call them Bleeding Hearts.

The four little flowers spoke to me in a wonderful way of a God who does things, both big and small, so beautifully. From God's wonderful hand comes a majestic mountain, a roaring sea, a thundering waterfall, a valley of green, a charming butterfly, a hopping bunny, a mighty lion or a quiet lamb. The bible of nature has so much to share and reveal of a God we call Father, a Creator who reveals His beauty in so many millions of ways.

We need to stop and smell the flowers! To take them in hand individually and to open our eyes and hearts to the message they all share so powerfully, of the One who fashioned them so beautifully and lovingly.

I've seen the works of the great master artists like Michelangelo, Raphael, da Vinci, and Botticelli. Their paintings are the manifestation of talent that makes one gaze in utter amazement. Rome and Florence are rich in their collections.

We need not travel to Italy to see great artistry for we are surrounded by the magnificent originals of the master artist of them all – the Creator. Each of His works is original and unique in its own special way.

Do yourself a favor. Pick a flower! Just one! And allow it to speak to you of God. †

The majesty of God stretches beyond the imagination

It was a hot day with temperatures in the mid-90s and a clear sky gave the sun all the opportunity in the world to keep things dry and hot. I paused on one of my calls to watch a rather small sprinkler challenge the power of the sun in trying to keep a bit of grass as green as the Irish shamrock. The contest wasn't too evenly matched and only the approach of evening would give the little sprinkler an opportunity to catch up a little and avert a carpet of brown instead of green.

That night, however, had a few pleasant surprises as God felt sorry for the little sprinkler and brought in the reserves to aid the situation. He started things off with a fireworks display of His own. Bolts of lightning streaked across the sky as if the Creator were taking pictures with a giant flash bulb. I wondered how many Eveready batteries would have been needed for that grand flash?

Then His drummers began to roll their drums. It was like thousands of buffalo stampeding on the range of the West. Then the rains came, in driving sheets while the earth opened its dry mouth and drank deeply of this fresh drink from the heavens.

I thought of the little sprinkler, standing in the rain sending forth its humble sprays of water in the face of the Lord's own watering system. The power and majesty of God is beyond one's furthest stretch of the imagination. We humans oftentimes get rather caught up with our various accomplishments and power, that is, until we pause to reflect on what the Almighty does just in the ordinary routine of a day's experiences.

Think of the water pressure and supply it would take to drop an inch of water all over Anoka County. It's humbling indeed to see what transpires in nature so easily under the hand of the One who holds the universe in the palm of His hand. Nature is a great prayer book and we need to read it frequently for the messages it offers.

God is always revealing Himself to us, attempting to capture our hearts as we travel the footpaths of life to the great Kingdom He has prepared for us beyond the stars. He spoke to me once again through a little sprinkler and a Minnesota thunderstorm.

Be on the watch and He will get your attention as well. ✝

Give to the Lord glory and praise

I watched with awe, wonder and a great degree of apprehension as the tornado funnel formed and moved down on the East River Road area. The view from the church parking lot was perfect and the funnel was moving north and a little east; with a little shift it could easily be over the church within a few minutes.

A lot of thoughts race through your mind at times such as that, one of which was seeing the church a wreckage of twisted beams, steel and bricks. In a few moments the labors of many months and years could easily be down the so-called drain.

The forces of nature have power beyond expression or realization, and there is little people can do but seek cover and pray for protection.

What indeed is God's power and majesty when you ponder on the works of the universe and consider that the tornado was only a small aspect of the total framework of nature?

It's a good, humbling experience and called to my mind seeing a young man recently flexing his muscles and giving the impression that he could just about handle anything that came his way. We all have our day when we feel like we are "king of the hill" and could take on anyone. Watching a tornado in action helps to keep one in their rightful place and a proper awareness of how strong we really are.

The 29th Psalm would be most appropriate to quote:
Give to the Lord, you sons of God, give to the Lord glory and praise,
Give to the Lord the glory due His name; adore the Lord in holy attire.
The voice of the Lord is over the waters, the God of glory thunders,
The Lord, over vast waters.
The voice of the Lord is, might; the voice of the Lord is majestic.
The voice of the Lord breaks the cedars, the Lord breaks the cedars of
*   Lebanon.*
He makes Lebanon leap like a calf and Sirion like a young bull.

The voice of the Lord strikes fiery flames;
The voice of the Lord shakes the desert,
The Lord shakes the wilderness of Kadesh.
The voice of the Lord twists the oaks and strips the forests, and in His
temple all say, "Glory!"
The Lord is enthroned above the flood;
The Lord is enthroned as king forever.
May the Lord give strength to his people; may the Lord bless his people
with peace! †

Nature speaks to the power of God

The question often arises in the various places of business, in schools, in society, in the country and the world: Who's in charge?

The storm last Thursday evening certainly made it quite clear WHO IS REALLY IN CHARGE!

Even the most powerful, the most proud and the cocky get rather mild and timid when it comes to facing off against the powers of nature. Can you imagine the engineering it would take to pour the amount of water over the Twin Cities area that fell from the heavens over the span of those few hours?

The Lord did it with great ease and didn't need any blueprints or sophisticated systems of hydraulics. How about those rolls of thunder and the sound of the tornadoes? Sounded like a few hundred thousand drummers in action. And those streaks of lightning? Not too shabby a display and on the spur of the moment at that.

We all need to sit back and admire the powers of nature. How tremendously they speak to the magnitude of God's power and majesty.

When we think we can push our little cart all by ourselves, it might be well to sit back and do a little reflecting on the great display of nature as it speaks of the Almighty hand that brought it into existence.

As one thinks of it all, it is rather amusing how we strut and glory over the little ant hills we erect in our brief passage of earthly journeying.

Yes, Lord, it was a great display you had Thursday night; it was worth some powerful reflection. Thanks for the nudge! ✝

Life has its splendid time in autumn

Fall is a wonderful time of year. It is so filled with color, splendor and the wonders of nature. The apple orchards have trees heavily laden with colorful red, juicy apples. The pumpkin fields are covered with a wide assortment of orange pumpkins that will find their way to delicious pumpkin pies or spectacular faces for Halloween. The meadows are blanketed with a dark-green carpet of grass. The maple trees, the most showy of all fall's colors, put on a grand spectacle of reds, oranges, yellows and all of the colors that fall in between. They look as if God artistically painted them with ten billion gallons of colorful paint. The corn stands ready for harvest with beautiful long ears, destined for many wonderful uses. The potato, the squash, the cabbage and the carrot are ready for harvest.

The wedge-shaped flocks of geese flying overhead, honking their way south, are a sure sign that tells us fall is indeed at hand.

How I remember those beautiful days of fall on the farm, when all of the various crops were gathered and stored safely in the barn, the granaries and the cold cellar to be used in the long, cold winter months ahead. When the wind blew bitterly cold and the snow piled high, how delightful it was to go to the cellar, or to the barns, and get some of the fruits of the previous fall's harvest. It made the long days and hours of labor during the summer worthwhile, as you sat back in the cold of winter and enjoyed the fruits of many months before.

Life also has its splendid time in autumn. In the closing years of life's journey on planet earth, God looks down on our lives and sees the fruits of our faithfulness and fidelity. The Sacraments we have received, the Masses we have offered, the prayers that have filled our lives, the good works that have graced our daily journeys, the suffering and the trials that seemed to be unending, all of these produce those rich, eternal colors of the Kingdom. They give a splendor to our life as it comes to a close, and then we discover how beautifully God will reward the faithful who have walked with Him during the course of life. How well we will understand God's great rewards and how these short years of earthly travel will unfold in the golden autumn of the Kingdom where the sun always shines, where the colors are always at their very best, where there is no chilling rainfall or cold blasts, where every day is a perfect day. The fruits of fall make the labors of summer worthwhile, the blessings of eternity, the ultimate of the autumn of life, make the spiritual efforts of a lifetime so very, very much worthwhile.

Nature is a beautiful book of prayer, and we need to read it regularly for the inspiration that it offers and to discern how beautifully it portrays the wonders of a great God we shall see forever. ✝

The powerful hand of God is something to behold

This past week my friend Bob and I toured the northern part of California. We drove along the coastal road and viewed the majesty of the Pacific Ocean with its powerful breakers crashing against the rocks of the shore. It was indeed a scene of the mighty forces of nature and the powerful hand of God that sustains them. One feels weak indeed before such a mighty force.

We drove into the forest among the giant redwoods of California. They stand tall and straight, reaching to the heavens as silent adorers before their God. We saw one of these trees, which was 386 feet tall with the lowest branch 190 feet from the ground. I believe the tree was forty feet in circumference and twelve feet in diameter. One feels rather small and insignificant in front of such massive grandeur.

I saw another stump that had been sawed in 1930. The tree began its life in 909 A.D. Can you image the things that have happened in the world since the tree first began to grow? It was a massive tree already at the Battle of Hastings in 1066. It was even larger when the Magna Carta was signed in 1215. It was a giant when Columbus discovered America in 1492 and it was even larger in 1776 when the Declaration of Independence was signed. The tree lived more than 1,000 years, rising to the heavens with its mighty trunk and giving witness to a God who fashioned such things with the ease of a little boy making a sand mound on the sea shore.

How proud we humans become with the little things that we fashion here and there; when we stop long enough to witness the great creations of nature, we see indeed how magnificent and glorious our God really is.

As we were going through the forest we stopped at a little gift shop and I picked up the following poem titled, "The Redwoods."

I'm sure you'll enjoy it and be inspired by it as I was. Read it, not only with attention, but with a prayer in your heart.

THE REDWOODS
Here, sown by the Creator's hand,
In serried ranks, the Redwoods stand;
No other clime is honored so,
No other lands their glory know.

The greatest of Earth's living forms,
Tall conquerors that laugh at storms,
Their challenge still unanswered rings,
Through fifty centuries of kings.

The nations that with them were young,
Rich empires, with their forts far-flung,
Lie buried now-their splendor gone;
But these proud monarchs still live on.

So shall they live, when ends our day,
When our crude citadels decay;
For brief the years allotted man,
But infinite perennials' span.

This is their temple, vaulted high,
And here we pause with reverent eye,
With silent tongue and awe-struck soul;
For here we sense life's proper goal;

To be like these, straight, true and fine,
To make our world, like theirs, a shrine;
Sink down, Oh, traveler, on your knees,
God stands before you in these trees.

–Author, Joseph B. Strauss
Builder of the Golden Gate Bridge

Weather can distract us from bad habits

With all of these cold days we have had in the past week or two, it would be my presumption that the devil doesn't like cold weather. Now this is just my perception; it is not the result of any comprehensive or analytic study that has been conducted by any research group which evaluates a lot of fine details and analyzes thousands of questionnaires. It is purely my simple conjecture.

On extremely cold days, if you'll listen attentively, what do people talk about the most? You will notice, without any in-depth evaluation, that it is the weather. It is a common denominator; everyone is experiencing it; everybody can speak about it; everybody can give their particular thoughts or analysis of it, because they too are going through it. Quite different from being asked to give an explanation of Einstein's Theory of Relativity.

Now here is where the devil comes into the picture. People are so busy talking about the weather, they don't have time to gossip about their neighbors, no time for uncharitable talk or any back biting or slashing at someone else's good name. Each has to share their story about the weather, how hard it was to start the car, what the wind chill was, the horrendous tie-ups in traffic with slippery streets and lots of other things, or how beautiful their car started after sitting outside all night, etc.

We're in the weather problem together, so there is a certain amount of release and relief in sharing the common misery. The Eighth Commandment, with its concern for uncharitable conversation, gets quite a rest.

The number two benefit of cold weather is that people are far more friendly; they speak more freely to one another, even complete strangers, which is understandable because they have a common interest at point. They can speak of the cold and know there is going to be a response. Whereas, if they asked someone about international or national affairs, or the market trends they may find someone who couldn't care less about the point of discussion and look with disdain at the conversationalist with a silent stare, saying, "What are you talking about, pal? Let me alone." Weather is another ballgame. They are all interested; they are living in it, they are experiencing it and ready to express their feelings and thoughts. We need a few more cold spells to get people out of their little shells and open them up to be greater conversationalists and more open and ready to engage others in conversation, wherever it may be. The devil doesn't like us interested in our fellow humans, our brothers and sisters under the Fatherhood of God.

Number three is a biggie. It gives the people the opportunity of reaching out and helping others, assisting in getting their car started, giving a hand to someone who is caught in a difficulty because of the cold. What a wonderful opportunity it provides to fulfill what the Lord says: *I assure you, as often as you do it for one of my least brothers, you do it for Me.* (Matthew 25:40)

On cold days you see people giving others a hand who under normal conditions wouldn't even think of it. There is a kind of comradeship in trial and tribulation, and people are inclined more to reach out, share and help.

So that is my little analysis of why I think the devil is very unhappy with cold weather. He is probably hoping the cold will pass and that warmer days will come, where he will have more of an opportunity of influencing his customers to walk the path of indifference to others.

You won't find the above analysis in any of the heavy theological tomes that grace the libraries of colleges and seminaries but only places like this, where a writer can indulge in flights of fancy and suffer no condemnatory sentence. †

God is the only 'real thing'

"Imitation" is a word that has a host of interpretations and meanings. The bottom line, though, is that it is not the real thing. Imitation gold, no matter how brightly it shines, is still not the real ticket and not worth lots of money.

Webster's dictionary says that "imitation" is "an artificial likeness."

When I was in California in 1988, I visited Universal Studios in Hollywood. There were 420 acres of a real working movie studio there where classic movies have been made since 1915.

They literally took you behind the scenes and there you quickly realized how much is false front with little behind. The scene of Moses and his people crossing the Red Sea was neatly accomplished with a couple of concrete retaining walls and some good flowing water. Watching someone bike over the top of skyscrapers was cleverly accomplished with a stationary bike and a beautiful backdrop of the city. It was nearly unbelievable to see what could be done with some clever photography. Giant monsters on the screen were little models easily moved by the hand of even a child.

It was a great experience and one that gave tremendous evidence of how passing, transitory and fickle the glitter, glamour and brightness of Hollywood really is.

It was a world of make believe and how passing it really all is in the presence of a God who lasts forever. As I passed through one movie set after another, my mind went back a few days earlier when we had visited Zion National Park. We drove down a dead end road for about twelve miles into an area called the "Cathedral." It was indescribable in its true beauty. There were solid walls of sheer rock rising hundreds of feet above the valley floor. Evergreen trees added a splendid splash of green color while animals of the woods roamed here and there. Birds sang their customary enchanting melodies while fluffy clouds paraded before the sun overhead.

This indeed wasn't Hollywood with its tinsel, make-believe and imitation. Our great God does things up in marvelous style, and how important it is that people prayerfully contemplate the real thing He has fashioned in nature, and thus place the imitation in its rightful place. ✝

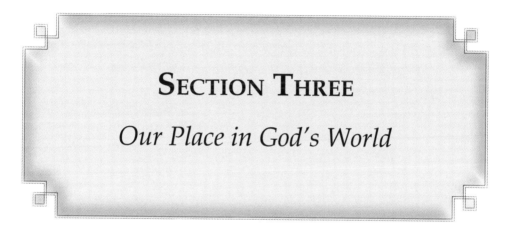

SECTION THREE

Our Place in God's World

Our Place in God's World

Those who expect to reap the blessings of freedom must, like men, undergo the fatigue of supporting it.

— Thomas Paine

Freedom is the birthright of man; it belongs to him by right of his humanity, in so far as this consists with every other person's freedom.

— Immanuel Kant

No man is free who cannot command himself.

— Pythagoras

We are all enriched with God's Grace for the purpose of developing our selves into His image and likeness. His life, which comes into each and every person's soul at the time of Baptism, is fostered through the other Sacraments by Grace, with its limitless potential from God. Grace produces varied and magnificent results in those who receive it. It helps each person in a very special and unique fashion. It helps one to be a better mother or a saleslady, another to be a good plumber, a good farmer, a good doctor or a good priest. Each responds in their own particular fashion and manner, each doing what God wants them to do in their particular vocation or way of life.

God also gives us free will, the freedom to choose to follow Him — or not. We probably all can point to instances in our world when those greatly blessed have directed their talents for evil purposes, with the result being that innocent people suffer. Free

WHATEVER YOU DID
FOR ONE OF THESE
LEAST BROTHERS OF MINE
YOU DID FOR ME

Mark Sanislo

will is part of God's plan for the world, like it or not.

Throughout my years as a priest, I have had the opportunity to travel to all parts of the world, witnessing first hand the suffering of those who aren't blessed with the freedom we Americans too often take for granted.

My trip to Haiti in the early 1990s impacted me far more than all my other journeys, however, for in Haiti I came face to face with the poorest of the poor, the "least" among us. Long before the 2010 earthquake devastated Haiti, Reiser Relief Inc., has been actively supporting the poor in Haiti.

When you finish enjoying *Reiser's Ramblings*, please take time to learn more about how you can make our world a better place by helping the world's poorest citizens by going online to www.ReiserRelief.org. †

God is the real power behind the scenes

I'm out on the highway and I just saw one of those Kemps Ice Cream trucks with a black and white Holstein cow painted on the side and then in large print it said, "It's the cows." Obviously they were saying, "It's the milk that makes the ice cream."

Being a farmer many years ago, I thought to myself, "Why don't they use a red and white Guernsey cow on that truck?"

Guernseys have, by far, higher butterfat content in their milk than Holsteins and if they are really talking quality, I would think they would be advertising the red-and-white cows. It's the cows who produce the milk and so naturally, we need to give them a great deal of credit for the marvelous product called ice cream.

Ice cream has always been a favorite dish of mine and I certainly have done my part to keep the industry going and very profitably. It is a magnificent dessert and with a few cookies, is a marvelous way of completing a day at midnight.

The real issue that I want to share and reflect on is: "It's the cows." What a spark this ignited in my mind!

Whenever we see something wonderful or spectacular in nature or man-made, whenever we see individuals perform with extraordinary and unusual talent and ability, there are two words that need to surface within ourselves: "It's God." He is indeed the real power behind the scenes. He is the reality that energizes everything that transpires, the spark that lights the fireworks of the world, the one who is behind all enthusiasm or movement of any kind.

How easy it is to give oneself the credit, when really the credit belongs to the giver of all good things, the magnificent and generous hand of God. As the Bible says: *Name something you have that you have not received.* (1 Corinthians 4:7)

There is no doubt that He is the wind beneath our wings, the hand that supports us and the one who gives and sustains life in every moment of our existence.

Behind every Beethoven or Michelangelo, behind every Vincent de Paul or Mother Teresa, behind every Henry Ford, George Washington or Abraham Lincoln, there is God. Behind every renowned surgeon, musician, industrialist or painter, there is God.

There is so very, very much that speaks to us of God, at every turn of the road, at every daily experience, with every moment of thought or word that flows from out of our mouth, there is the great reminder that God is behind it all. How important it is to recognize His presence, to live under His wings and to know that He loves us with an infinite love.

Wonder of wonders that such a God is ours.

For ice cream, "It's the cows," but for us humans, "It's God." ✝

Fr. Reiser blesses the new church building.

Let's look past the daily
crisis to see the big picture

Thankfully, Coca Cola is going back to its old formula and we can avert another national crisis. With the news coverage given this terribly significant fact and the response of so many, with some even storing hundreds of cases, it was taking on the dimensions of another cataclysm in our social structure.

I was only five years old during the 1929 Stock Market crash that caused financial ruin for countless numbers; then came the drought of the early 1930s; in the late 1930s, Hitler, Mussolini and Stalin brought war and bloodshed to Europe; Pearl Harbor in 1941 roused the fury of America and nearly four years of bloodshed followed; VE and VJ days followed that and post war years experienced a major shift in gears. The wars in Korea and Vietnam brought many anxious years to Americans who were personally involved. The early 1960s brought the Second Vatican Council and a good measure of turmoil in the Church. A change is usually difficult, especially in areas where people have experienced very little change or alteration.

The last ten years have witnessed a fluctuating economy with high interest rates and unemployment percentages that create dark overtones in the lives of millions.

Yes, there have been many tense situations and crises over the past three-quarters of a century.

All of the above have adequately prepared me for this latest crisis on the American scene – should Coke really dump the old formula and go with a new one and create nearly mob hysteria?

In an era when half the world goes to bed hungry every night and thousands die daily of starvation in Ethiopia and India, it seems rather sad that changing any formula of a soft drink should provoke more than a couple lines on page thirty-nine of the local paper. We live in an age when trivia occupies so much of our attention and big issues like where did we come from, who made us, where are we going after death, and what is life all about, get very little of people's time, let alone much mention in the daily press or on the TV channels. †

Trivial matters tend to distract us from focusing on what's important, such as lifting children out of poverty.

Freedom involves responsibility and answering for the decisions we make

July 4th is always a great day in the United States of America, as we celebrate Independence Day, the day America declared its independence from England. The Revolutionary War was a bitter struggle but one that our forefathers considered most primary so that the colonies could act independently, without the domination of a power from across the sea.

Freedom is a basic quality of the human person, for we are created with an intellect and a free will. We have a will that can make its own decisions or determinations. Whenever that freedom is taken away, there comes a burden to the individual. Over the years I have visited many, many individuals in prison, and how often they have said to me, "You can give us the very finest of foods, carpet our cells and make them as comfortable as possible, but when you take away a person's freedom, you have taken away one of his greatest possessions."

Freedom is a marvelous and wonderful gift but it also entails something called responsibility. It means that when we make choices, we have to answer for them, that we are responsible for them. We are responsible for our actions, for our choices, and we need to pay the consequences for them. We need also to endure the consequences, not only of our own free choices, but the choices of others.

These reflections were prompted by something that I experience many, many times per month. How God is often blamed for many things He should not be blamed for! Someone is killed in an accident, and especially if it is a child, people will say, "Why did God do this to us? Why did He take that little child?"

The reality is that God doesn't kill little children or deliberately cause accidents, but He does allow people to exercise their freedom of choice. If someone chooses to drink and then drive and kills a number of people on the highway, it is not that God wished this to happen. It is that He has allowed an individual to make their own choice even though others will need to pay the consequence for it.

Hitler, Stalin and Mussolini made many choices during the era of the Second World War and from those choices, millions and millions died. God can interfere with the free choices of humans but ordinarily does not. If we want a freedom, such as that of choice, then we must pay the consequence for it, whether those choices are made by ourselves or by others.

Chickens, birds, cattle and fish have no free choice. They are directed completely by instinct. Would we rather be a chicken — or a human who assumes the responsibilities for our actions?

Privileges involve responsibilities, if you have the one you must accept the other. People die of starvation and malnutrition in undeveloped countries because the developed countries of the world have not assumed adequate responsibility and made the choice for sharing their super-abundant wealth.

It is not that God does not provide. As He provides for the sparrows on the tree tops, He will also provide for humans. But humans must assume the responsibility of sharing and reaching out to those who are in need.

Before we blame or criticize God for this or that particular difficulty, it might be well to look into the situation and say, "Was this a result of my own decision-making or the decision-making of some other human?" Let's not be blaming God too quickly. He is not accustomed to interfere with human decisions; He can but most often does not.

As we celebrate Independence Day, let us remember that freedom involves responsibility *and* answering for the decisions we make. †

Honesty renews the spirit

There are beautiful stories about honest Abe Lincoln that thrill the heart and makes one yearn for those days when a person's word was their bond and integrity was taken for granted.

Last week, Wednesday, I received an envelope in the mail and inside was a short note saying, "Greetings. The other day we were undercharged at your restaurant. Enclosed is $6. God love you. Walt."

The note rekindled my awareness that there is still honesty in the world despite all the tales you hear of people being bilked and cheated.

How little Walt knew that thousands would hear about his honesty and integrity. It would be like a little ripple that grows to a giant wave, touching the hearts of many.

Life is full of many little things that, at first, seem to be rather inconsequential but they end up having a great impact on many, many people. When we all put those little things together, it changes society, changes the very community in which we live. It takes individual little raindrops to make a great rainfall, as it takes little individual acts of honesty here and there to create an atmosphere of honesty, integrity and responsibility.

Be always on the lookout when you can invest a little energy, a little time, a little concern to make your area of life overflowing with greater personal integrity and it can help change this world into a better place to live. At first observation, the act may not seem very big or powerful, but we never know how far its reality will travel and influence the hearts of others.

Be a part in helping spread the good wave of honesty and integrity. Each little action helps people to rekindle their faith, their confidence that humans are made to the image and likeness of God, and the more we live like God, the more harmony, trust and confidence people will have in one another.

I had thousands of different contacts at the State Fair. I saw people come and go at the Dining Hall, both inside and outside. There were tens of thousands of faces and people, but among them all I shall never forget the man who sent the $6. I couldn't identify his face. I only know that his name is Walt and he is an honest man. †

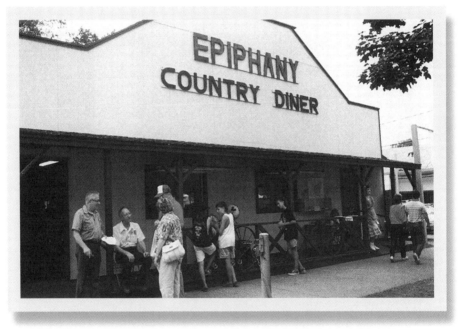

Visiting with folks outside the old Epiphany Diner.

As our homes go, so goes society

There is always a great cry in our modern day about preserving our natural resources and how necessary and vital that is for our own human preservation. Over the years, we have been extremely careless and have raised havoc with all of the wonderful things of nature that God has given us. Lakes were polluted, rivers were filled with sewage, forests were laid waste and our very atmosphere has been attacked ruthlessly and has opened us to many serious consequences. So the cry has gone out that we must conserve those great gifts of nature that God has given us.

Conserving natural resources begins with you and begins with me. It demands a respect and a reverence for all of God's creation, it demands a sincere effort at recycling and all of the other procedures that are aimed at preserving what God has given us.

What is being said of our natural resources might indeed also be said of one of our greatest resources, the family. As our families are being torn apart in a host of ways, society suffers some devastating consequences. When our homes are not peaceful but racked with quarreling, fighting and disputes, we have serious consequences on those who grow up in such a situation. Those raised in the dysfunctional family carry scars for many a decade.

As we see violence growing more and more in our cities, while safety is continually at a higher risk as every week and month proceed, we all need to take serious note of how we can offset this violence and savagery that is so rampant in all directions. As with the preservation of nature, we all need to begin with ourselves and within our own homes to counteract violence. We need to start at home to promote more peace, more togetherness and more love.

If we want harmony on our streets and in our cities, we need to have harmony within our homes. Each and every one of us needs to strive with all of our hearts to promote peace, togetherness and unity within that essential element of society, our home.

As our homes go, so goes society. As the number of family breakups continues to increase year by year, is it any wonder that we are seeing more and more violence and disruption on our city streets?

Let us strive to bring a little more peace, a little more harmony within our own household. Be more understanding, more forgiving, more generous, more gentle.

Be conscious that every reform begins first with the individual. If each person does his or her part to be more peaceful and loving, this love will extend, in magnificent fashion, to all of society. †

The persuasive power of prayer

There is an old saying, "There are more things wrought by prayer than this world dreams of."

The truth of that statement is often demonstrated but one of the more dramatic testimonies to it was when radical reformer Boris Yeltsin was inaugurated as the first popularly elected president in Russia's 1,000-year history. The ceremony held at the Kremlin in Moscow was filled with religious and pre-revolutionary symbols.

The millions over the past decades who have fingered their rosaries for the conversion of Russia now see the beginning of the fulfillment of their heart-felt dreams.

Fifty years ago the illustrious Bishop Fulton J. Sheen said that we needed to pray for the conversion of Russia and that Russia would then be the great nation for the conversion of the East. That prophecy by the famous radio and TV personality is beginning to unfold its truth.

Slowly, but surely perhaps, the world will learn that peace and extraordinary happenings within the hearts and minds of people come about not by guns, nuclear power and force, but by the gentle and persuasive wind of prayer. It is prayer that reaches into the depths of the human soul and heart, and aids the conversion of the false philosophies to the truths of almighty God.

In the inauguration of Yeltsin, he was blessed with the Sign of the Cross by Alexei II, Patriarch of the Russian Orthodox Church, who said to him, "By the will of God and the choice of the people, you are bestowed with the highest office in Russia. We will pray for you."

Alexei II even appealed to Yeltsin to pay mind to the "Law of Christ" and told the new Russian president, "You have now a great cross to bear." The patriarch called on Yeltsin to encourage a spiritual rebirth of Russia after decades of religious persecution and asked him to help restore churches, cathedrals and the Russian countryside.

Yes, God is very much alive and His power is moving throughout the earth. If you want to be a tremendous instrument in the world in which you live, become a person of prayer. In the quiet of your home spend some time with the Lord in prayer and reading of Scripture. Find time

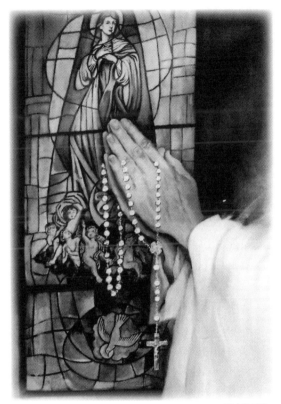

Mark Sanislo

to make a visit to the chapel and perhaps to extend that visit soon to an hour a week of Adoration. Be fervent in your reception of the Sacraments and your attendance at Holy Mass, and through these you will become a tremendous power in changing the world for God.

Prayer does work and so we must fight the forces of evil with a spiritual force, and that force is the power of prayer. ✝

It's a great Church that holds us all

My old Irish Pastor, Father Finn, who went to the Lord at age ninety-five, had a great saying, among many others: "It's a great Church that holds us all." The diversity of its people enriches the universal framework of our Church.

I thought of this Sunday as those five lovely Sisters of St. Peter Claver made an appeal for the missions of the world. A real international flavor prevailed as three of them were from Poland, one was from Italy and one from Vietnam, and they were asking Americans to help people in Africa and other distant lands.

Nearly 2,000 years ago, Jesus asked his followers to teach all nations and how fittingly those words were ringing in our ears this past weekend. It's this kind of spirit that helps us all take a step closer to the union of all people in a family we love.

When we reach out beyond nationality, race, color or creed, we are indeed building up the "Kingdom" over which Christ will reign.

One could easily become a little melancholy in reading the daily press of all the violence over the world. So much print is given to the killings, the battles, the strife, the insurrections, etc. That is why Sunday's experience of the love and concern you all showed in the appeal of the Sisters was indeed very heartwarming.

It gave me lots of assurance that the forces of good are still way ahead of the troops that toll the bells of despair, destruction and death.

Sunday saw hands reaching into pockets and then across the earth to touch the lives of peoples we shall only see in eternity.

It's a great Church indeed that holds us all and the Lord is still very much in control. You made me very proud on Sunday with your gifts to the missions. Thanks so much! †

Jesus is the model for all volunteers

Who was the greatest volunteer who ever walked this great earth? None other than Jesus Christ, the great Galilean. He gave His all for the good of each and every one of us. From one end of Palestine to the other, He walked with the twelve apostles and everywhere He went, He gave of Himself for the needs of others. The driving force within was an uncompromising love.

Jesus is the model for all volunteers, the spirit of doing for others, not because one has to, but because one wants to, reaching out to the needs of others, to make this a better world. Serving others because the rewards are not necessarily found here on earth but in the great Kingdom beyond the stars where a hundredfold is measured out in reward.

Churches and many institutions could not carry out many of their ministries or missions if it were not for their volunteers. Here at Epiphany, volunteers have made Epiphany what it is: a thriving, healthy, vibrant Christian community.

Over these past twenty-four years, tens of thousands of dedicated parishioners have made Christ a living reality in our community. Their names are beyond numbering, but the Lord knows who they are.

The great Galilean walks in your shoes as you use your time and talents to extend His Kingdom. †

The more we study, the more we understand how little we know

There is an old saying, "It takes lots of people to make the world go around." When we look at life, what a grand assortment of people there is, each with their own particular specialty in life, each trained in a particular fashion to do with great excellence one kind of work. During the past week, I was really alerted as to how fortunate we are to have individuals who have developed great excellence in what they do.

My brother needed brain surgery and what an assurance it was to visit with the neurosurgeon who had done many of these surgeries. He outlined in detail and with great clarity what he was going to do. When we questioned him about possible heart problems my brother was susceptible to, he said, "Well, that's not my field, and I'll have a cardiologist on hand to take care of those particular needs." Another question prompted the following response, "That's the role of the anesthesiologist and he'll handle that in great form." It was a powerful comfort to know that these three specialists would be standing side-by-side giving their best for someone I love.

The night before, on the way to the hospital, my car developed problems and so I pulled into a service station, for God knows I wouldn't be able to handle that problem, no matter how simple it was. After about ten minutes, the mechanic gave me a complete evaluation on what was wrong, what was needed and how it could be corrected. He had the right machines and he knew how to use them, what buttons to push and what results to look for. I was lucky to have come upon him.

A couple of days later, I found myself sitting in the dentist chair and my dear dentist with great precision took care of a number of fillings and he did it with great perfection in an area that certainly isn't that large. I often wonder how they can get all those instruments inside one's mouth and do what they do. (Now don't be saying that I've got a big mouth.)

The next day, I'm sitting down to dinner and enjoying all these beautifully prepared foods that have been done so tastefully by the housekeeper. Thank God we have people who know their way around the kitchen and can put things together with the professionalism of a French chef.

There was lots of correspondence to take care of during the day and so I merely put it in front of the secretary and with jet speed, she rolled out those letters and other correspondence with great accuracy and promptness.

I slipped into the washroom to freshen up a bit and it was clean as a whistle with smells as fresh as a new day in spring.

Computers are certainly far from my competence. I needed a new program to put some things together, so the computer lady whips it out in short order and the job is done very quickly.

Repairs were needed here and there in the school and church area and maintenance dispatches the tasks in short order.

And so in just a few days, here was this wide variety of people, all with different skills and different expertise, to handle the duties, the needs at hand. What fools we are when we think we know it all, or that we even have a small corner on the knowledge in the world. The more we study and the more we pursue knowledge, the more we understand how little we know and what a vast range of knowledge there is within the world. All of this knowledge is a mere reflection, a shadow, of that Infinite Knowledge and Wisdom that is God. God is Infinite Truth, and in Eternity, with each passing moment of existence, He will unfold before us the Truth that will excite us beyond expression. Heaven will have much to offer, so I get more excited by each passing day, as to what God will share with us when we enter the Kingdom. †

Freedom is lost when
free people don't take it seriously

Next Wednesday, July 4 is Independence Day and it's 208 years since our Founding Fathers drafted that historic Declaration of Independence to give America the liberty that if fought so hard to win.

Freedom is a much cherished possession and one that we often take for granted while so many millions of people throughout the world live under tyranny and know only repression and control.

Often we don't appreciate gifts we have until they are taken away. Those who have gone blind can tell us much of what eyesight is all about. A broken leg I suffered about fifteen years ago taught me a real appreciation for the ability to walk.

What is this all leading to? The school board election of May 15, when only 4.5 percent of registered voters (in two districts) took interest and time to vote in that particular election.

Education is a tremendously important part of our children and young people's development. In the classrooms of today are fashioned the citizens of tomorrow. The policies of education are in turn directed by the school board who is, in turn, elected by us voters.

This little rambling is not a commentary on any or all of the candidates, but a little jolt to arouse the voters to a greater sense of responsibility to take all elections seriously.

Freedoms are often lost when free people do not take their freedom seriously! †

Use freedom in a manner that pleases God

In our modern day, it is certainly almost the most famous of all walls, and they call it the Berlin Wall. It stands as a glaring and terrifying symbol of what Communism is all about, a philosophy that destroys every vestige of freedom and places chains around people's bodies, minds and hearts.

I stood and looked at a sentry station manned by two soldiers of East Berlin. Just a few months earlier, gunfire by soldiers from this lookout position killed a nineteen-year-old youth as he was crawling to the freedom of the West. A black cross intertwined with barbed wire marked the spot. His picture and a short commentary graced the front of the cross.

The Wall was erected in May 1961 after hundreds of thousands of East Berliners had fled to the West to escape the slavery of Communism. In one night, the barbed wire was up on ninety-six miles of border and in three days, the Wall was built.

Thirty-five percent of Berlin's families have been split by the Wall. What great anguish this brings to these families with some living in freedom and others under the tyranny of the Soviet hammer and sickle. Travel back and forth is monitored with great scrutiny and some family members are kept behind to assure the return of others.

As you walk along the Wall and see the many crosses marking those who attempted to escape to freedom and had been killed by Wall guards, you gain a deeper appreciation of how valuable freedom really is.

Can you imagine a wall down Hanson Boulevard separating the people of Coon Rapids with all of the above realities?

Be grateful for freedom and use it in a manner that pleases God and serves the welfare of our fellow humans. [†]

Freedom is a basic right of humanity

When you experience something continually, one is inclined to take it for granted. Those who have never been blind can never really appreciate what it means to be able to see. Those who hear have difficulty knowing the trauma of being deaf. Those who have always been able to walk have little awareness of what it means not being able to freely move from one place to another.

We who enjoy freedom have little consciousness and awareness of what it means to live in a country where there isn't that beautiful reality of freedom.

China is one of the few remaining strong, socialistic governments in the world. The government owns all the land, the properties, the homes and businesses. Wages are low, and the motive and incentive for advancement are very weak. You live in government housing, you travel on government buses, your employer is the government and all wages and conditions of life are set by the government. There is a low level of trust and confidence in other people because one has little awareness of who is a strong party member or not.

When you finish college your field of study does not necessarily determine where you will work. Two of our guides had degrees in engineering, and our national guide had a degree in international law, but they were not pursuing the fields in which they were schooled but the area of work the government determined for them.

The Tiananmen Square revolt of 1989 was basically led by university students of China, who were fed up with the system and saw no future of where it was going. Unfortunately the revolt was crushed by the government and thousands were killed, but the spirit and philosophy within the hearts of the students was not killed, and there will be a restlessness within their hearts until real freedom comes to China.

In recent years, China has opened its doors and numerous joint venture businesses are developing. In these the Chinese government and foreign investment firms are sharing in building new business ventures.

Tourism has become the second major industry of China. As more and more Chinese people encounter the peoples of the world, their dissatisfaction with socialism will grow.

Freedom is a marvelous quality and it provides the opportunity to live where you wish, do as you wish, build if you wish, work in the particular area of human endeavor that you wish, and to come and go as you desire.

God created humans to be free to make their own determinations and not be controlled or dominated by another.

Americans won a bloody and costly revolution back in 1776, but it was a war to defend and gain one of the most basic qualities that humans enjoy— the quality of freedom.

We need to appreciate freedom, cherish it, use it well and not abuse it.

When freedom is exercised according to the norms that God has given us — in the Ten Commandments and in the teachings of Jesus Christ — it is enriching, enhancing and ennobling. It profits not only the individual who enjoys it, but all others with whom the person comes in contact.

Appreciate your freedom and use it well. ✝

Bigotry is contrary to Christ's message

Jesus was on the mountaintop with His eleven Disciples, and His final words to them were very pointed, very meaningful, and all inclusive. He said: *Full authority has been given to Me both in Heaven and on Earth; go, therefore, make disciples of all the nations.* (Matthew 28:18-19)

Those were some of the most significant and important words that Jesus ever spoke. He was charging His Disciples to go into the world and make disciples of all people. None were to be excluded. All were to be invited to membership into His family.

The Church was not to be for one group rather than another group, or one race rather than another race, or one people over other people. The Church was to embrace everyone, regardless of race, color or origin.

What a terrible monster is any form of prejudice that we may have toward any people or groups of people. Any form of bias is completely contrary to the message, the teachings of Jesus Christ. We call ourselves "Christians," meaning, "followers of Christ." Therefore, we must be willing to embrace all people as our brothers and sisters in Christ.

When the Disciples asked Jesus how to pray, it is very significant that the Lord's first two words were, "Our Father." God is the Father of all, regardless of the nation we come from, the continent we live on, or the social status we find ourselves in. The color of our skin, the nature of our accent, the educational or economic status we may enjoy, makes us no better or less than anyone else who rubs shoulders with us as we walk the pathways of life.

We all need to look into our heart and soul and examine our thoughts as we approach the varying people that populate the face of the earth. In our thoughts and actions, do we see others as equals, and that they are loved by God the same as He loves us?

The word "inclusive" is a word that we all need to embrace

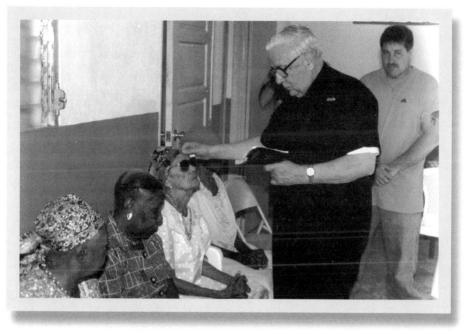

Fr. Reiser blessing the elderly in Haiti.

in our own particular life. In our lives, are we willing to reach out and touch the hearts of all those that we meet or know in our experience of life?

Physical appearance, intellectual ability, social grace, or being articulate in speech, do not make us any better than anyone else who comes within our circle of living.

Racism, bias, and prejudice, are ugly realities in any nation, culture, community, or within our own lives. Being male or female makes us no better or less than the other gender.

Heaven will be a wonderful experience because all will embrace all others. We will truly see how all are children of the same great Heavenly Father, all brothers and sisters of Jesus Christ, all loved, being loved and loving in a similar fashion.

Why don't we begin living that way here on earth? Life on earth should be an anticipation of the life hereafter. ✝

Good triumphs; evil is destined to fail

The concentration camps of the Second World War are a blot on human history that can never be erased. They are a terrible recalling of man's inhumanity to man. They tell the story of the depths to which the human heart can sink in hatred, reprisal, animosity and revenge.

The Nazi regime was built on the philosophy that there is no God, there is no future life, there is no spiritual soul and the code of conduct was based on what is good for the State or what is bad for the State. All this set the criteria on how all actions were to be judged. Is it any wonder that we then witnessed the terrible things that transpired? For if there is no God or afterlife and rightness of action is determined by the State, we have opened the door to most anything and everything transpiring.

The German concentration camps of the Second World War are a tragic story of suffering and death. They also tell the story of a human spirit that frequently cannot be crushed, but rises up in the face of horrible atrocities and remains unconquerable. It gives evidence that good does eventually triumph and evil is always destined to fail. Our God in Heaven is supreme and all the adversaries to good are ultimately destined to destruction and failure. †

Holding candidates to unreasonable standards

It's another presidential election year [1992] and from now until November it will be certainly a regular item on the front page of the newspaper, on television and radio. All will carry the latest on the presidential candidates and anyone who runs will certainly be subjected to a close analysis and a careful scrutiny of every aspect of their former life. If there is any possibility of uncovering even the least bit of scandal or dirt, it will certainly be done with every possible skill in the investigative process. Many seem to relish the opportunity of uncovering any shady parts of the person's previous life.

If our Lord had done the above, He certainly would have been deprived of many excellent and splendid workers for His Church. St. Paul's record was certainly far from praiseworthy when he was the infamous Saul of Tarsus. Mary Magdalene had her time of certainly not enjoying a very elegant reputation. Our modern day Matt Talbot, soon to be canonized, walked the road of the alcoholic for many a year.

None of us have lived a perfect life and I'm sure as we look back over our years of experience, there are things we regret having done and would certainly like to do over again.

There are perhaps some excellent leaders out among the people that could provide much for our country but perhaps are afraid to come forth for fear of the devastating scrutiny that might be placed on their life.

Perhaps a little more effort could be given to examining their priority of issues? What are the principles and priorities that the candidate holds sacred within their life? What are their concerns for the country's poor, for racism and segregation? What is their vision as far as creating a society of justice, equality, and fairness for all? What are their goals? What are their plans for addressing the social problems of our world where millions starve or live at a level below reasonable human standards?

St. Ignatius and St. Francis of Assisi very dramatically changed the atmosphere of the world in which they lived, and an examination of their earlier lives indicated individuals who were far more concerned about personal well-being than the things they so enthusiastically and energetically embraced later on.

The point is simply that people can change and alter their lives. They can rise beyond the mistakes of the past and walk the straight and narrow path of goodness and justice in the years ahead.

I have no particular candidate in mind in writing the above but just wanted to share some thoughts, reflections and ramblings on an issue I believe needs discussion. Do we often throw out the candidate with the bathwater? †

Politics could use some rules of fair play

The primary is over and there are less than two months to the general election in November. All will indeed be happy when the final ballots are cast and we shall breathe a sigh of relief that the mud-slinging will be over for at least a couple of years.

When you hear the devastating remarks that candidates make concerning one another you sometimes wonder whether we have any candidate that is a worthwhile individual. The many negative comments that have been spoken create fear and hesitation to have any of the candidates in public office.

There must be some alternative to this continual bashing that takes place one election after another. Perhaps there should be some ground rules laid as to what is allowed and not allowed, for even in the field of sports there are rules that are set and maintained. In baseball it is not uncommon for players or managers to be ejected for unfavorable comments or conduct. Perhaps some rules of fair play could be established on the state as well as the national political levels so that there could be a reasonable approach in this whole question of election campaigning.

Despite all of these negatives, we still are a long mile ahead of the Communist style, as we found in China, where there is no real freedom of expression.

No matter how upset we may become with a particular system, when we look around, there always seems to be one that is less appealing. Our democratic approach surely has provided us with many magnificent benefits over the more than 200 years of American history. However, that certainly does not mean we can't clean up the system and make it a little more acceptable in the eyes of civilized human beings.

In our own personal lives, we might each examine whether we operate a mud-slinging machine towards others by speaking of their faults and failures or do we see their good qualities and scatter perfume and beautiful roses? There is a world of difference. †

Your labors have special significance in the world

Cy is a stocky, well-built Irishman who arrives at the building site of our new church Monday through Friday at 7:00 a.m. His craftsmanship will be looked upon and admired long after the writer of this little column has gone to the happy hunting ground beyond the stars. Cy is one of the bricklayers on our new church. From our first meeting, I knew he was someone special and a person I would cherish seeing often. His smile is as big as his shoulders are broad and his laughter tickles your eardrums more effectively than a feather as it rolls so beautifully from his happy personality.

I encountered him one day as he was moving to the construction trailer for a coffee break. "Pretty soft!" I commented. "I wish I had an easy job like this."

Quick as lightning was his Irish wit as he responded, "Father, your vocation is to be a priest and my vocation is to be a bricklayer. To each his own way of life."

No wonder there is joy in his life and merriment in his speech. Cy knows that his bricklaying is a special calling; for him, it is a vocation in life. With love and responsibility, he lays brick upon brick, for he performs an important task in the arena of life's various activities. Now he builds a temple for a Lord who called him to lay brick, but with every movement of his trowel, he silently but eloquently inspired others to see their labor in the work-a-day world as having a special calling and significance.

There was another craftsman who was a carpenter, who also took pride in his work and understood the nobility of his vocation; they called him Joseph of Nazareth and now he enjoys a great spotlight in the Lord's Kingdom next to a fair lady called Mary and a foster son called Jesus.

What is your vocation — housewife, waitress, secretary, machinist, truck driver, assembly line worker, salesman or clerk? Take pride in it. Do it with nobility, honor and dignity. Remember, the Lord reads the heart and not the job description. †

Construction underway at the new Epiphany Church.

Work hard and be
proud of your vocation

My daily visit to the construction site is always an exciting and enriching experience. To see each of the tradesmen executing their particular talent, whether it is electrical, plumbing, carpentry, iron worker, heating, finisher, etc., reminds one of what a diversity of talents there are in this great world of humanity. Each person knows his field with a very special expertise and each does it with pride and nobility.

It takes all kinds of talents to make this old earth of ours run so smoothly and it's a humbling experience to watch these various craftsmen at work doing their tasks so proficiently and easily. It calls to mind those days when you were fresh out of high school or college and the ink was scarcely dry on the parchment or sheepskin and, my, how we thought we knew it all and had it all together!

It takes a few years of knocks and bumps, a few grey hairs and a few sagging muscles to know that we often aren't half as smart as we think we are. The sooner we learn those lessons in life, the easier the path becomes!

So, hats off to everyone in your particular area of work. No one knows it all, so do well whatever you do and take pride in it. ✝

Our skills come from the Almighty hand of the Creator

There was an incident that happened out on the construction site of the senior housing that was indeed very inspiring as well as amusing. On the site was a large backhoe that scoops up five yards of dirt in one scoop. The operator has a fantastic skill and it is a real pleasure to watch him operate this many, many ton machine. He does so with the expertise and precision of a surgeon in an operating room. He moves this huge piece of equipment about as if it were a little toy.

But a real highlight came last week when one of the students of the school kicked a soccer ball out on the construction site far beyond the playing field. The operator of the backhoe saw the dilemma of the student, who wouldn't dare venture out into the construction area, so, he maneuvered around and picked up the soccer ball without picking up a bit of dirt and then swung back and shot the ball back to the student with a magnificent maneuver of the scoop. He looked like Magic Johnson flipping in a basket from center court. Years of operating the machine have given him absolute command of his machine and he operates it with the grace of a ballet dancer.

There are so many different talents among people, such a wide variety of gifts and skills, that to ponder them sets one back in utter amazement, for each skill comes from the almighty hand of the Creator who needs to possess all things that He shares with us humans.

How stupid pride is, to think we know it all, or to think we have a corner on the world's intelligence. When you survey the many different talents and the extraordinary manner in which so many use them, it is indeed a very humbling experience, and you begin to realize how little each of us knows individually and what a small part we are in that vast arena of intellectual activity.

We all need to treat with deep respect the gifts and talents of others, to praise God and commend the people who use them, knowing that they all come from the generous hand of God.

It takes all kinds of people to make up this great world of ours, and when we encounter each and every one of them, we should have a deep respect and reverence for them. They are manifesting what God has given them in a very special and singular manner. Those who think they know it all really need to be pitied, for failing to realize how little they really know in that vast arena of knowledge.

Yes, the backhoe man really knows his job and knows it well. I need to get out there one of these days and climb up on his machine and tell him what a real expert he is. †

Receive the Lord
with a heart full of love

There are many thoughts that run through my mind as I give the Holy Eucharist to people day after day. It is a real inspiration to see the great variety of hands into which we lay our Blessed Lord. Some are frail and some are strong, some are young and some are old, some are wrinkled and some have cracks filled with grease for they are hands of a hard-working man making a living for his family.

Each set of hands preaches a great message of an individual's love for their God. Their hands tell a great story of the individual, but there is something even more important, and that is what is in the heart of each of these people, as they come forward to receive Holy Communion. The externals are one thing and they tell a great story, but the internal tells another story that I trust is just as beautiful and wonderful, hearts that are filled with love and devotion for their God as they come to receive Him one more time.

All of this was prompted from a little note I received from one of our parishioners, Sharon Christian. I would like to share it with you. It tells a great story and is filled with inspiration for each of us.

"As I was going up to the Lord's Table, I saw this beautiful little girl going up to receive our Lord Jesus. Her little hands were cupped together just so and she looked so proud and reverent. Then, I noted that her little hands were stained from markers she probably used to make a Father's Day card for her dad. What would people think? Then, I realized that Jesus doesn't really care how we look when we come to Him or even if our hands are stained from work. We should receive Him with our hearts as full of love for Him as this little child's. This is the lesson I learned today, as I watched my daughter receive Our Lord with her little stained hands." †

Stay attuned to your dependence on the Lord

Someone gave me a clever plaque that reads, "Those who think they know it all are very annoying to those of us who do." The plaque is all in fun, but how sad it is when any human feels they have all the answers and are the last word on any particular issue or subject. Every day I come across people who are absolutely geniuses in their particular field. They do their job with extraordinary expertise and with the ease with which I would read the morning paper.

Last Thursday morning at about 7:20, I heard what sounded like a strong bang and then the lights went out in my room. The Lord knows I wouldn't even know where to start looking for the trouble. The power company was called and in a very brief time they were on the job, and in short order they assured me that they knew the exact spot where the feeder line from the street had been short-circuited causing the bang. A backhoe was quickly on the scene and they told me that the power would be flowing in about twenty minutes. I marveled at the speed, efficiency and the expertise with which all of this happened. They knew what they were doing and did it in excellent time.

When I go to Mercy and Unity Hospitals I see the wonders done in surgery by well-trained hands and heads. There are heart and brain surgeries that we would never have dreamt of years ago.

Our computer system continually amazes me and I admit that I don't even know where to turn it on. Mechanics fix my car, well-trained seamstresses keep my clothes in order, an excellent cook keeps me nice and plump, not to mention the thousands of others who do their job in an excellent and fantastic matter.

None of us are independent. We are so utterly dependent on the many, many people that surround us and how sad it is when

Fr. Reiser celebrating Mass in Haiti.

we fail to acknowledge that dependence. How ridiculous it is when we maintain a cocky, self-sufficient attitude of life. There is so much in life's experiences to keep us humble and aware that we aren't a very big cog in the great experience of human life on planet Earth. What fools we are when we think that we are the great movers, planners or directors.

Yes, Lord, keep me humble and keep me aware of how dependent I really am, not only on all of those who surround me, with a magnificent support system, but ultimately on You, O God, from whom all things come, from whom all things proceed, and from whom all things are sustained in existence. If You were to withdraw Your power, I would cease to exist, for all things are ultimately made from nothingness, by Thy Divine and Almighty Power. ✝

Teamwork produces amazing results

Living on the farm provided many wonderful lessons for life. They were taught by experience, by living and not through reading books. Experience is a wonderful teacher and from it we can gain many important directives for life.

When I was a boy, the power used on the farm was principally horse power, and a good team or two of horses were really the "bread and butter" of life, because you depended on them to carry out all of the work on the farm from plowing, to harrowing, to planting, to cultivating and harvesting. They were literally part of the family, because if they became ill, or had a sore hoof, we would be in dire trouble. We always referred to them as a team as they both were needed for any of the major tasks. How vital it was that they always pulled together. If you were cultivating corn with a riding cultivator and if one horse was slower than the other, or held back, or didn't perform its task, you were in real trouble, and were constantly moving your feet to not root out all the corn. Tasks became doubly difficult if they didn't pull together, for then it was up to the farmer to make the necessary adjustments. What a joy, and how much easier it was, when they walked step-for-step, shoulder-to-shoulder, down the row, each doing their own individual part, and not expecting the other to carry any of the load that wasn't theirs.

In any organization, undertaking, or enterprise, teamwork is really one of the most important of all elements. Each having a particular task and each doing it with all of the energy and enthusiasm that they can muster brings any undertaking to a successful conclusion.

We at Epiphany have been blessed many thousands of times by the wonderful teamwork among our parishioners. I was thinking the other day of the thousands of people who make Epiphany "purr like a kitten," the thousands of volunteers that so generous-

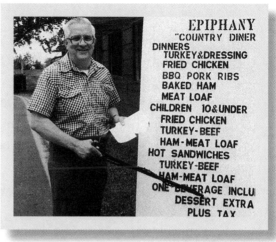

ly and lovingly do a variety of tasks that are beyond numbering, each using their own particular talents, time, and energies in a very loving manner. Our parish could not accomplish all of the various tasks and ministries that it fulfills if it were not for those who volunteer, and when they volunteer, to work as a team, pulling together, putting their shoulders to the task and doing it with love and dedication. The results are amazing.

If you really want to see an example of teamwork, just be at the State Fair Diner for a day. When you see seventy-five people pulling together, each doing their own particular job, the result is a magnificent variety of meals, service and happy customers. With 3,000 to 4,000 people going through the dining room doors in a single day, cooperation is an absolute and teamwork a necessity. There is an old adage I heard from my mother very frequently and it went, in English, as follows: "Many hands make any job easy."

Teamwork produces wonders and achievements beyond expressions. When there is teamwork in a family, everything runs so much more smoothly, each doing their own particular tasks with joy and enthusiasm. Even a small child can do his part to make the operation run easier and smoother.

These thoughts all unfolded as I recalled the team of horses on the farm. How well they worked together and what wonderful results they produced. There were many furrows plowed, many a road cultivated, many rows of crops harvested, and the horses did it all with wonderful teamwork. Let's always follow their example. †

Work is part of human life

Labor Day is a day that all Americans look to as a day off, a free day from the regular job they go to day after day. It is a day to honor the laboring man, and the laboring man is not merely the one who uses the strength of his arms and legs but also those who do office jobs with various skills. Work is part of man's life, going back to the days of Adam and Eve and the Garden of Paradise. God said to our first parents: *In the sweat of thy brow thou shalt eat the bread*. (Genesis 3:19)

Things would not just be dropped in their laps henceforth but they would need to work and toil with mind and body to maintain their sustenance of life.

Work is a marvelous dimension of man's life for when people are out of a job they look forward to the day when they can again be gainfully employed. They need to work not only to sustain themselves and their family, whoever they are responsible for, but they need to have some activities to keep them busy. You know the old adage: *Idleness is the devil's workshop*.

When people retire it doesn't take long before they are searching for something to do, a variety of volunteer projects or other things to occupy their time. Labor Day has also another dimension it gives to all who are paid for their work, a gentle nudge to fulfill their duties and responsibilities in a spirit of justice and righteousness. If one is paid for eight days labor, whether mental or physical, they have an obligation of fulfilling the responsibility of giving to their employer a rightful return for what they have been given. One finds a great measure of injustice where people work maybe six hours and loaf for two, but still are paid for eight, or where coffee breaks are doubled and lunch hours are extended unreasonably.

All need to look into their lives to discover whether there is a just return for what they are justly receiving. There are so many opportunities of injustice in the workplace that much depends on the honor, integrity and justice of the worker. Expense accounts can be padded so unfairly, and it is so easy to rationalize and justify actions with expressions such as "it's a big company they won't know the difference." We all need to look into our lives and maybe ask the big question: What would Jesus do if He were in my situation? He is always the perfect standard, the model for all actions.

There is also the question of workmanship, excellence in that which we do. How easy is it to do a second-class job rather than give the effort for doing the very best we can in the situation at hand? In my varying tours through Europe, one reality that was very noticeable was the excellence of workmanship in construction of the churches and how people took great pride in making something with the greatest perfection and skill possible.

Labor Day has rolled around and you had your extra day off and now are settled back to work. Perhaps you could think about some of the thoughts that have been offered here, and see whether they are of any value in your own particular job. †

Rules for game of life are set at family table

The men's conference this past weekend certainly emphasized in magnificent fashion the value of home life. It is in the home where the future of a community, a nation and the world is fashioned. We are only as good and strong as our homes. When our homes are happy and strong, when they are religious and good, values are communicated and society is on an excellent and straight path.

The adults of tomorrow's generation are the children of the present generation. As sons and daughters are formed and fashioned within our homes, thus the world will go. As a tree is inclined, so it will grow. If the tree is crooked from the early months, thus it will grow for the length of its life, unless there are some radical measures to straighten it.

The religious destiny of an individual is fashioned so powerfully at the mother's knee. Our faith life is fashioned and the truths of the Lord are communicated best when the mind is young, open and sensitive to all of the varying impressions. The Blessed Mother spent thirty years fashioning her Son, Jesus. It was there within the household of Nazareth that Jesus was groomed in the practice of virtue and good habits. The Son of God did not descend from Heaven as a full grown man, but He was born as a baby like all of us and thus the process of formation was gradual at the hands of Mary and Joseph. Jesus learned the basics of human life and the varying habits of religious life and of sharing with others from Mary and Joseph.

The true success of a mother and father is not realized in their accomplishments outside of the home but in those things that they accomplish in fashioning the little ones that God gives them. In the home, we should find the greatest schooling environment in spiritual values.

We live in an age in which the achievements in business, a profession, worldly success, or social position are often more important than creating a splendid, excellent home life. For women, there is certainly nothing more important than the duties they assume around their home. The duties in society or in the workplace, necessary as they may be, need always be secondary to that of fashioning and forming the future adults of the world and the saints of Heaven.

I grew up in an age in which building home life was far more important than the style or size of the house. The house provides shelter and all of the various elements that we need in living, but it is the home that reaches out into eternity itself by the lasting impressions that are given to the sons and daughters growing up around the table.

Our era seems to be one in which there is a competition for seeing how many athletic teams we can be on or extracurricular activities involved in and consequently parents become cabbies for their children. They drive here, there and everywhere for dozens of games and activities and the big game of life, centered on the family table and the family room, are ignored. Meal time together gives way to the fast food restaurant and sitting alone in front of a computer or a television.

Have we lost our values and given in to a modern society that is built around consumerism and materialism? There needs to be a wake-up call in America and a return to that which is lasting and forever: the true values of family life. ✝

We face a host of problems when we go it alone

As violence erupted in Los Angeles in 1992, I'm sure the world at large was following, pondering and wondering. And indeed, they had a right to be doing all of those things, because, this was not the America whose soldiers fought in Korea or in Vietnam or the Gulf War to protect the rights of individuals. We were in those conflicts because each person is a special individual created by Almighty God and we fought for those people's rights, dignity and privileges.

America has in many instances, portrayed itself as a knight clothed in armor and riding a white horse ready to protect the right of the individual and to see that the unjust aggressor is held at bay, not permitted to carry on ruthless aggression against anyone.

I wonder what thoughts were running through the minds of the people of the world as they watched American men who were to represent law and order beat another individual who was down and out. How would they feel when they see a so-called court of justice close its eyes to ruthlessness and let the perpetrators of violence go free? I wonder what they are thinking when they see thousands of citizens take the law into their own hands and perpetrate acts of violence, beyond description, burning, looting, attacking, killing, as if injustice is to be dealt with by more injustice and violence is to be responded to by more violence? The nation on the white horse with the shining armor has some deep problems within its social structure. And things in River City aren't perhaps as good as many might imagine.

Is it that our great country is morally bankrupt? A country that has a million and a half abortions a year; a country which has seen an alarming breakup of the family structure through separation and divorce; a country which has lost its reverence and respect for sexuality; where there seems to be the convergent principle that if it looks okay, it's alright to do; that freedom of sexual experience is appropriate for our modern era and waiting for marriage is really being old-fashioned. Dishonesty runs rampant even among the highest levels of government and those who were entrusted with a sense of justice and honesty seem to have forgotten the meaning of the words. Are we really falling apart at the seams because we have become corrupt from within?

Is there perhaps a rather obvious reason why our whole structure of morals is going down hill? Consider that half of the population of the United States doesn't bother to go to Church all year long and among those who are members of a particular church only half of them go on a regular basis. Is it any wonder that we are in the state of affairs that we are in?

God created this great universe of ours and each one of us. He gave a set of guidelines called the Ten Commandments and when we follow those rules, things will work harmoniously. We need to follow the book of instructions for anything that we own, whether it's a motor, a car, a watch or anything else. When you follow the instructions, things run smoothly and with great ease; but when you disregard the directions and go it on your own, you soon discover that there are going to be problems and lots of them. We as humans need to follow the instructions our Creator gave us, and when we do, there is harmony, there is peace, there is order, and there is charity and all of the other qualities that God wishes us to enjoy.

What can we do after what's happened in Los Angeles? We can resolve to make our own lives as good, as wholesome and religious as possible. We can live by the Commandments that God has given us. We can follow the principles and the rules of life that Jesus gave us; then each of us becomes a better person and society becomes a better community in which to live. Each person is very important, each needs to do their part, for criticizing others won't make society any better—but perhaps add to the disorder.

When I am healthy spiritually and morally, then you will be

healthier spiritually and morally just by our association. Let's start a wonderful trend, a trend towards a good and wholesome society, in which there is love, charity, kindness and peace — not violence and destruction. We, as a country, will then become that "knight in shining armor," riding our white horse to making the whole world a better place to live. †

Christianity an expression of togetherness

Is the glass half full or half empty? It's all a matter of perspective, how we look at things. Do we see the positives or do we see the negatives? We can look at a rose bush and see the thorns and the sharp edges or we can see the beauty and the glory of the radiant red rose. It's all what we're looking for or pursuing.

For many centuries, the Christian religions emphasized their differences and how they disagreed one with the other and this of course made for more division, more separation, and more disunion for the followers of the Lord. In the last twenty-five years however, there has been a change of perspective and attitude. Rather than looking at the differences between the varying religions, we are beginning to look at the togetherness, the ways in which we are similar. We call it by a very classy word called "ecumenism." This has resulted in a lot of togetherness, a lot of good feelings, and certainly the great virtue of charity has become more apparent between all of the different religions than it was forty-five years ago.

A couple of weeks ago, I preached at a Lenten service at the Coon Rapids United Methodist Church just down Hanson Boulevard. It was a wonderful experience and certainly gave me a great feeling within to know that there could be some real closeness between the two Churches. The reception I received was warm, cordial and very enthusiastic. I felt like one of them. On my day of ordination forty-two years ago, I would have never dreamt that such a thing would ever happen; but here it was in reality.

Then, last Sunday evening, was another grand step forward in which the Coon Rapids United Methodist Choir joined with the Epiphany Choir in presenting a very beautiful and marvelous Sunday evening concert. It was performed with excellence, devotion and most of all, with love. One of the high points of the evening was when Pastor Grant Tanner, of the Coon Rapids

United Methodist Church, sang and played a musical composition he had written on the life of Christ from Saint Mark's Gospel. It was most inspiring, very moving and certainly done in a wonderful musical style.

Wonderful fellowship followed the musical concert and certainly the sharing and fraternity that was enjoyed was one that sent everyone home feeling a little better and a little prouder. Two Christian churches had joined hands, hearts, and voices to honor their God and to extend His Kingdom a little more surely throughout the earth. †

Gratitude isn't measured by what we have

A couple of weeks ago, I had a wonderful experience when I spent some time at Mary Jo Copeland's Sharing and Caring Hands. Some of our Epiphany people were serving the dinner and the place was jumping with activity.

It was a heartwarming experience and one of those special times in life that make you really glad to be alive. There was an extraordinary atmosphere of joy and a real festive mood prevailed. There was an accordion player providing some good foot-stomping music and a few responded very well to the invitation.

They were celebrating St. Valentine's Day and the menu was chili, sandwiches, cookies and coffee, which was for many of them like a Thanksgiving dinner. There was no shoving or pushing in the food line; in fact, they just gracefully moved in when the line became short. Everyone was friendly and enjoyed chatting for a bit. I was visiting with a man when Mary Jo came over and I said to him, "What's her name?"

He flashed a big smile and said, "Angel!" What a magnificent tribute. She returned a big smile and gave him a gentle kiss on the cheek.

I thought of Christ's words: *Whatsoever you do for the least of your brothers and sisters, you do for Me.* (Matthew 25:40)

I looked at the many people in the shelter, dressed in clothes that were not tailored for them on Fifth Avenue in New York. They weren't a clean-shaven group and not much after-shave lotion was in the air. But there was something special I noticed as I moved around the shelter. Despite the cold day and all the hardships, these people endure from day to day, not a single person complained or said, "Isn't the weather cold or isn't this or that terrible?" Rather, there was a very positive, joyous and delightful spirit in the hearts of all.

I left the shelter and stopped at North Memorial Hospital to see a sick parishioner. I met a nurse on the elevator and gave her a cheerful greeting. Her response was, "It sure is cold out and I have a whole shift to work."

I was tempted to say, "You poor darling, why don't you change places with the street people and then see your attitude."

Often those who have so much complain the most and those who have so little are so very grateful for what they have.

Yes, it was a wonderful day and the people at Sharing and Caring Hands made it even better! ✝

Christ's life radiates
through the work of Mother Teresa

The Christophers have a marvelous saying, "Better to light a candle than curse the darkness." That being true, I wonder how many millions and millions of candles Mother Teresa caused to be lit through her magnificent and marvelous life. She literally lit the world by her love, compassion and kindness. Everywhere she went, the people felt God's presence. The power that flowed from her life originated in her adoration and reception of the Eucharist. She was a woman who knew Christ so personally that His life radiated through her every action and word. As the Sun illuminates the Moon, so Jesus Christ was the burning light within the life of Mother Teresa.

She moved as easily among kings, queens, Popes, presidents and great leaders of state as she did among the poor of Calcutta she loved so dearly. Each held specialness no matter what they did, or didn't do, in life because each was created to the image and likeness of God.

People come and go, but the likes of Mother Teresa come seldom and rarely, with the magnetism and power of person she possessed. Her humble and simple dress, her unpretentious speech and her humble manner made her very special among the people of the earth.

Several centuries ago, John the Baptist issued a clarion call along the banks of the Jordan River, directing attention to the new Messiah — Jesus of Nazareth. People like the great Herod stood in awe in his presence and listened with great attentiveness to the words that flowed from his lips. Our century has had another John the Baptist, different in style but with the same direction, calling people's attention to Christ, to His way of life, to His teachings, that we might in turn embrace them as our own, namely, Teresa, the Angel of Calcutta.

There is an old saying that "apples fall not far from the tree, that children are an expression of their parents and teachers," and so the sisters in Mother Teresa's order give beautiful expression of the teacher from whom they learned the lesson of Christianity.

I encountered the sisters of Mother Teresa firsthand while I was in Haiti. They operate an orphanage for children dying of malnutrition. Half of the children in Haiti die before the age of four, so you can imagine the number of little ones the good sisters take care of. A visit to their orphanage was a heart-wrenching experience, to see dozens of little ones in their cribs, with their little bodies severely ravaged by malnutrition. Shortly after our arrival at the orphanage, a young mother brought in her baby and one of the sisters said, "In less than three days this child will be dead unless extraordinary methods are successful."

When you picked a child up, they held on for dear life because of their need for love and closeness. The work of the sisters in the orphanage is beyond expression in its value and goodness.

One of the most inspirational Masses I have ever offered was in the chapel of the orphanage. The sisters, along with some of the little babies they cared for, were present with our group. It was a moving, touching experience and the Lord God certainly was close at hand.

We also visited a home for adults who were terminal, men and women by the dozens, lying on beds with sheets white as snow, cared for with a love that was beyond expression. Their stay on earth would indeed be short. The sisters had me anoint a few dozen of them who were close to death.

This was only one area in the world where Mother Teresa's sisters share their love. I believe they have 500 missions, all of them inspired, motivated, touched by this great woman called Teresa. Who could possibly measure the good influence she has had in our twentieth century? God's grace and power can

Mark Sanislo

work wonders when the human individual allows itself to be an instrument, as Mother Teresa did so beautifully. Our hats are off to her, our voices echo her accolades and we thank God for the magnificent manner in which she said "yes" to God. †

Visit to Haiti compels relief effort

My trip to Haiti last January will long be remembered. Over the last thirty years, I have had the opportunity to travel much of the world and never have I seen poverty in such stark reality as I experienced in Haiti. They speak of the Third World countries that have tremendous needs. I would say that Haiti is in the Fourth World.

We visited Cité Soleil, a Port-au-Prince slum, where a quarter of a million people live without running water, a sewage system and scarcely any electricity, a scene that is unbelievable. The sanitation problem is beyond expression, the shortage of free fresh water is unbelievable, and the lack of food is tragic, especially when you see so much food wasted here in bountiful America. With no running water, people need to go to a central supply point and carry home their water in five-gallon buckets. At one water center 26,000 people come on a normal day to get water. This is only one of the locations. Many people live alongside garbage piles that are unbelievable. While we wonder about which food we should choose for a meal they can look forward to the same diet day after day, rice with a bean sauce over the top, and they are very fortunate to have that if anything.

As we went to this area several times during our stay, I thought to myself, the animals on our farm years ago lived in far better circumstances than do these human beings. We who live in such comfort cannot imagine the situation that these people endure day after day.

The seven of us who made the journey all experienced the same traumatic impressions and we have a compelling need to do something to alleviate at least some of the misery, poverty, hardship and trauma.

We easily spent the $10,000 that was given in the second collection on Christmas day. It was spent as follows:

Four thousand dollars was given to the Sisters of Mother

Haitian children carry life-saving water to their homes in buckets.
Reiser Relief Inc., covers the costs to deliver fresh water
six-days-a-week to the poor living in Cité Soleil, Haiti.

Teresa. We visited two of their homes, one that takes care of the malnourished infants and dying children, the other was a home for dying adults. Both visits were very traumatic. The effects of malnutrition are devastating.

We gave $2,000 to a young married man, Loll Jean-Phillipe, who runs a school for 175 children from the slums who are in very desperate need. He does a fantastic job with the little he receives and our check was certainly a day brightener and offered much encouragement in his selfless dedication to the little ones.

Father Horelle Fleuriscat, who works in the mountains and travels by mule and foot, received $1,000. The money will take care of his budget for six months. He educates 1,000 children with volunteer teachers. The smile on his face was unforgettable as I gave him the check.

One thousand dollars went to Yvette Papillon who runs various places for the destitute. We visited one which is called her nutrition center where dozens and dozens of people come each day for extra nutritional needs, various vitamins, medications and so forth. She has been cooking with charcoal to feed the many who come to her, some of our donation will go toward two gas-burning cooking units and tanks of propane which will make her situation much easier.

With $400, I was able to buy a one-room home for a man and wife with four children. Certainly nothing very spacious but it is a place to call their own and lay their heads. Another $200 went to a man who takes in homeless children he cares, educates and provides for. The other $400 went to various needy men, women and children.

We visited Leogone, which has a place for abandoned women, away from Port-au-Prince, run by Sister Claudette. There were nearly 200 women who were brought there from the streets of Port-au-Prince, and from other areas. Sister Claudette and a few helpers care for them with the love that is Christ Himself. The meals were simple but nourishing. The beds were clean and the sheets as white as snow. There was so much love being extended that it touched your heart to do something positive to help in some way.

We gave $1,000 to Sr. Claudette; she does a fantastic job caring for these people, showing them much love and attention. Their need for more facilities was apparent at a moment's glance, so our group agreed to do something about it. We have decided to build another residence for abandoned people, about a mile from the present one, which would have sixty or more beds and would provide adequate and decent living conditions to people who are not experiencing them. The cost of the project will be $175,000, which we see as a very attainable goal, especially when you see the tremendous need.

I shall also remember that area very well, because it was there that I fell and scraped my leg and subsequently got an infection

More than half of all Haitians are unable to read or write.
Reiser Relief Inc., pays teachers' salaries in two Haitian schools.

in my leg that I have battled for ten months. It is nearly all healed now, but the duration of the healing has been a constant reminder of my need to so something for these poor people. Perhaps the healing was delayed to impress upon my mind that their suffering never goes away and the only termination for many is death. Surely we can do something to alleviate their hardships in life. The reward for those who help the poor will certainly be most bountiful on the last day; the Lord said a hundredfold.

I assure you, as often as you did it for one of my least brothers and sisters, you did it for me. (Matthew 25:40)

The trip to Haiti was an experience of a lifetime, never to be forgotten. The dedication of the people who serve these very, very needy people is beyond expression. They are certainly serving Christ in a most magnificent and glorious way. Your generosity gave you a very personal part in their works of love and their caring for God's neglected children and adults. ✝

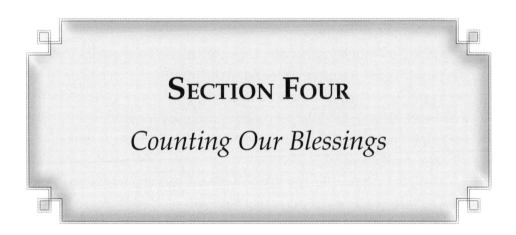

SECTION FOUR

Counting Our Blessings

Counting Our Blessings

The Lord and I were out on Communion calls one morning when it occurred to me what a difficult situation He is placed in time and time again, situations and decision making I am thankful I haven't faced.

I thought of those many, many times that He is approached by His people here on earth to respond to their particular wishes or needs and how hard it must be to make the decision as to which way to go. How frequently people pray from opposite sides of the fence. There are thousands of examples that I could cite, but perhaps I will share just a few:

There is a fellow who has just laid a lot of sod, the whole yard, back and front, and so he prays that God will send some gentle rain so that the sod takes root very nicely and he won't need to water. But someone else is having a marvelous wedding celebration and they would like sunshine to be showered down upon the bride and groom. Quite a dilemma to face!

Or, consider those wonderful men who bought beautiful new snowplows and they would like to fill their billfolds with the green stuff and so they obviously pray for at least a few feet of snow. Others pray for beautiful dry roads and no snow shoveling.

The fuel oil people and the garage men love the cold weather; it's great for business and certainly helps them to balance the budget, whereas those who are hard pressed thank God for every warm day and the savings they will have in lower fuel or car repair bills. And so it can go, on and on and on.

What's good for one is bad for another. That which is a real plus on the ledger for this individual can be a real cause of concern and promote a negative balance for another. What pleases one brings a frown to another. While one is exalting and rejoicing over this or that, another is having an extremely difficult time.

Yes, the Lord must really have a tough time trying to keep us all happy and content, answering what we consider to be urgent needs. He must be really frustrated at times listening to each of us wanting our own little way.

Over the years, I have learned in my prayers to just leave things up to the Lord. Pray, "Lord, you know what's best and you know the circumstances of the situation and where it's all coming from. Decide what's best; I know that's exactly what you always do because being all good and perfect there's no other way you can go."

Then, whatever comes your way, just accept it and know that God sees the whole picture. He has the vision that reaches from one end of eternity to the other. This approach brings a lot of inner peace and contentment.

As I look back over varying things that I thought were best for me, I soon discovered that what I thought was best was far from best and had I received it, things would not necessarily have been to my advantage.

Adults all feel that they have more vision and more perspective than a child, and rightly so, for they should have gained something from years of experience and a good measure of education. How much then must we trust the decisions of our loving Father in Heaven?

Have no question of His infinite love for you; consequently, trust that whatever He decides on your behalf is surely for the best. †

No person is an island

It has been six days that I've been in my bedroom, on my bed, and not taking a step on my left foot. Antibiotics come to me at regular intervals and even more frequently, hot packs on my leg to draw out the poison. It has been a tremendous learning experience and one I will not soon forget. We take so much in life for granted and we never really appreciate thoroughly so many, many gifts that we have so generously been given by God — until we lose them. It is then we begin to really appreciate, cherish and value them.

We are very rich people when we have the gift of seeing, hearing, talking, and using our hands and feet, gifts that we would not very quickly sell for many millions of dollars.

Being incapacitated makes us very very dependent on others and we quickly see how we don't row our own boats very well by ourselves. How utterly dependent we can become on the generosity, love and kindness of others. No person is an island, independent of the rest of the humans who surround him. Our dependency on others is certainly far greater than we personally share with others.

The Lord slows us down on occasion and reminds us of the great saying in Scripture: *What do you have that you have not received and if you have received it, why do you glory as if you have received it not?* (1 Corinthians 4:7)

Some may think, if he hadn't gone to Haiti, he wouldn't have fallen, wouldn't have the infection, and wouldn't be laid up for this period of time. Was the trip worth it? It surely was. My little inconvenience and pain is nothing compared to what these people in Haiti suffer day after day, seeing their children die of malnutrition and not being able to give them what they would love to give them of the various things of the world.

Can you imagine living in grinding poverty day after day, facing the daily menu of rice with bean sauce on top of it, without any hope for change or a different menu? Living where sanitation is often nearly unheard of and having water means carrying it in five-gallon pails? A poverty with no hope of alleviation and a future that holds nothing but the same grinding sufferings of today?

The scenes of Haiti will always remain fresh within my mind and heart. There will always be a determination to alleviate a little bit of that suffering as best I can.

All humans are made in God's image and likeness, and they deserve to be treated with dignity, honor, and to have at least the essentials of livelihood.

My bed is clean, Rae's food is magnificent, the nursing care given by Kathleen is excellent, the room is warm, the water is cool and clean, the sanitation is excellent and the power company keeps the lights burning brightly. Hundreds of thousands in Haiti could not say the same.

Patience is being tested in the slow process of healing but we all need to take our share of knocks in life. As I look at my past years, the Lord has been extremely generous, kind and good to me. I need to say, "May God be praised in all things." ✝

Everything we have is an expression of love

We all take so very much for granted. Considering the many, many gifts we all enjoy, how often do we pause to reflect and say, "Thank you, God," for them?

That is why Thanksgiving is always a grand and glorious time in the year to kind of shake us up a bit and make us more sensitive, more conscious of the wonderful things we possess. As I sat down to a wonderful turkey dinner, last Thursday, I couldn't help but think of all those people in the world who are grasping for just a bit of food to keep them from starvation. They are satisfied with anything they can get to keep them alive, while we become so picky about this or that, about our likes and dislikes. Thankfulness is one of the great prayers that should fill our hearts. Next to the prayers of love and adoration, it is the greatest of all movements of the heart and soul toward God.

The more thankful we are, the more we notice that everything we have is an expression of love, a gift from God, and whatever we accomplish, is merely utilizing those things that have been first given to us.

Seeing someone who needs to use a wheelchair reminds me of how blessed I am to be able to move one foot in front of another. The white cane being moved so cautiously in front of another person makes me look twice at the beautiful sights around me and say, "Thanks, Lord, for my eyes with which I see."

How many millions there are who, day by day, go through life without one of their five senses, or even several of them.

The greatest gift, however, is the gift of faith. It gives me direction and purpose and goals in the day-to-day activities of life. It leads me to the great mountain of God and reminds me that it is only as I pursue God's ways, goals and teachings that I am really achieving my purpose and reason for being here on planet Earth.

The center of our faith is the Holy Eucharist. The word "Eucharist" comes from a Greek word meaning "thanksgiving." The

Lord wants us to be people thankful to the great Father of us all who cares for our every need.

Thankfulness leads to many other virtues and certainly not the least of them is humility. Humility is recognizing that what we have and who we are, the gifts we enjoy and use are given to us by a good God. They are loaned to us by God and are ours to use in the manner and fashion that God would desire.

Every day we need to be more like that one leper out of the ten who returned to give thanks to the Lord. However, we are often like the other nine lepers who didn't return. We need days like Thanksgiving to be tugging at our hearts and touching our minds to say "thank you" far more often.

So, as I look at turkey bones waiting to be made into delicious noodle soup, and as I gaze at the pie tin now empty, I remember a day that has been a positive experience because it has been a day when God has touched my heart a little more to say, "thank you," more frequently and to be grateful from the depths of my heart for all of His goodness and kindness and generosity. ✝

God gets blamed for more things than one can imagine

Who gets blamed for more things than anybody else? How many think, "I do?" One often hears people say, "Well, I can never do anything right." The answer to the question is God. After nearly fifty years of priestly ministry, I can say without any reservation that God gets blamed for more things than you can possibly imagine.

Often, when an individual has a severe illness or contracts some disease or has a serious lung problem, cancer, arthritis, heart trouble, or name a dozen others, one of the first things you frequently hear is, "Why does God do this to me? I say my prayers, I lead a good life, I go to Church, I receive the Sacraments, I carry out all of my varying Christian responsibilities, and now I have this critical or terminal illness."

I can truthfully say I have heard such statements thousands of times over these past fifty years.

The truth is, God doesn't send us diseases, illnesses and the like. If modern medicine knew what caused cancer, it would obviously use the appropriate measures to stop it. God doesn't look down and say, "I'm going to give this person a little something to be concerned about," and then implant some cancer virus. All the various diseases are a reality among humans because of our human nature and they will be around until the last human has breathed their last breath.

We need to know that God does not normally interfere with the natural process of human nature. If we contract a particular virus, bug or whatever else causes illness, we are going to suffer the disease. If I encountered a particular virus, God isn't going to reach down and snatch the virus out of my system. He easily could do it, but He doesn't normally interfere with nature. I had a dandy cold and laryngitis last week and I certainly do not believe that God looked at me and said, "It's high time that priest had a few more afflictions and difficulties to know what it is like to be sick."

God is a loving Father and He doesn't do that type of thing. He does know, however, that suffering will be good for me, make me more grateful for good health, and give me an opportunity to offer my affliction to the suffering Christ on the road to Calvary.

I will never forget, some years ago when a three-year-old was killed on the highway. She had strayed from her yard and walked into the path of a truck. The mother was a Christian and was, of course, deeply crushed. When her Christian friends came to the wake, they all told her, "God wanted your little one in Heaven as a special Saint and therefore took her." It sounds rather good at first flush, but when you think about it, it really doesn't set too well. The mother became extremely angry at God and quit going to Church for many years. Her Christian friends, though meaning well, had given her some very bad advice. God doesn't look down from Heaven and see where He can pluck an innocent child from the earth to add another Saint to the chorus of singers in Heaven. The child unfortunately ran out onto a busy highway and God had nothing to do with her being killed.

Does God interfere with nature on occasion? He can. Does He frequently? I would be inclined to say no. Does He send death and illness to people intentionally? I would think not, but He certainly permits the forces of nature to act in their normal, natural course of events.

For some reason, we seem to have lots of tornadoes in Anoka County. I can't explain what causes a tornado but there are meteorologists who can. When we have them, I don't think God is looking from Heaven saying, "You know, I'm going to get those people in Anoka County. They deserve to be shaken up a little more and brought to their knees." If that were true I would be inclined to say to the Lord, "Now, why don't you pick on some of the other eighty-six counties in the state?" We don't have hurricanes in Minnesota for the simple reason we don't live near the ocean. Why should we be blaming God for every hurricane that sweeps the seaboard and causes destruction and the loss of life? Hurricanes are a natural reality on ocean seaboards.

So the next time you or one of your relatives gets an incurable illness, or suffers some fatal accident, or is involved in some particular tragedy, I believe it's good to be rather hesitant to start blaming God. Nature will continue to be nature, accidents will continue to happen and humans will be humans. In all of these areas, we will find lots of explanations when these tragic moments occur. It's best not to blame God. ✝

God loves each of us uniquely

Travel is a wonderful experience and a great privilege. It gives one a great awareness of the tremendous diversity among people and their ways of living. Each has its own unique culture and traditions, and when one sees the wide range of diversity among people, it gives an insight into the infinitude of Almighty God. Each culture has only a small portion of that vast wealth that is the God of Heaven and Earth.

Traveling is a humbling experience. As you make your way through a large foreign city, whether it be in Europe, Africa or the Near East, where no one knows you or few understand your language, you could fall over dead on the street and cause very little stir indeed.

As we go on through life, we oftentimes create a high degree of self-importance and think that we are rather vital in the workings of the world. That self-importance is quickly deflated as you enter into a foreign land, among peoples who do not know you. You begin to realize that the little square piece of property we may live on is infinitesimal in comparison to the whole Earth.

Whenever I travel and see all of the different people I have never seen before, I think to myself, "On judgment day, all of them will be there." To realize that God knows each one of them, as He knows me, individually, specially, helps me realize He loves each human with a unique, infinite love. He embraces us all in a very special and magnificent manner.

What a stupid thing pride is, or any form of vanity.

Humility, indeed, is knowing who we are in relationship to Almighty God, and that everything we have and everything we are is His generous gift to us.

Travel makes one more tolerant of all of the differences among people and it teaches very dramatically how stupid is prejudice of any kind. No nation or people are really "king of the hill" nor has a country a right or privilege to dominate another.

Some countries have more natural resources than others, but these are not for their own enrichment or opportunity for power. Rather, they are the opportunity to serve and to share with others. †

Travel makes us more tolerant of peoples' differences.

Be grateful for the blessings of each day

The University Hospital receptionist graciously said, "Jack's on Station 31, Amy on 41, and Deanne on Heart 3."

I saw Jack Turner first. A strange disease was threatening his eyesight and the possibility of blindness haunted his every waking moment. Amy Peterson, at fifteen, was meeting the challenges of cancer day by day. Sixteen-year-old Deanne Backes was having a leg amputated the next day.

A lot of drama was packed into that hour of visiting and praying. I didn't mind the walk back to the car some blocks away because it felt great to have two legs to walk on. The hot sun was no trouble at all because it made it possible to see all the wonders about me. It felt good to have a tired body because being able to work is a tremendous gift.

Like everyone else, I can take a lot for granted. We moan over a lot of little inconveniences and other annoyances and lose sight of the big things God gives us. The next time you have to park an extra block away, thank God you can walk it.

Pick up your Bible right now. Isn't it great you can see to read? Oh yes, why not give someone in the house a hand? It's super to be healthy and well! †

A wonderful gift is the gift of faith

It was a few years ago that I sat down one morning to have breakfast and, as was my custom, I spread the morning paper out on the table next to my cereal to look at the front page. To my dismay, I couldn't read any of the paper. It was blurred, cloudy, and I couldn't distinguish any of the words. There was panic in my whole being and I thought, "Am I losing my sight? Am I going blind?"

A thousand different thoughts raced through my mind as I looked at the paper with blurred vision and the inability to read. Was this my destiny for the rest of my life, that I would spend my years with the inability to read and the possibility of perhaps losing my sight? Some hours later, my vision returned, to my great joy and wonderful surprise. I didn't know the meaning or the explanation, but later found out the answer from a good eye doctor.

Ever since that memorable morning breakfast some years ago, I have had a deeper and keener appreciation of what it means to be able to see, to read and to use the eyes that God has given me so generously. I am less inclined to take them for granted, and I daily appreciate the ability to see the magnificent beauty of the flowers, the flying geese of fall, the sunsets and sunrises, the fleeting clouds, the smiling faces of others and the countenances of so many people at the various states of joy or grief.

Over these past forty-eight years of priesthood, I have witnessed and been close to the death of hundreds, seeing their bodies become still after their souls went to God. I spoke to many, many families about faith, the leaving of the soul, and how we need to look beyond the physical and be transported to the realms of God. In death the soul, the spirit, is gone to be in God's company forever, and the shelf of the body is laid to rest someday to await the touch of God, of a new creation, the infusion of the soul and then the whole person is filled with eternal life.

Our body is indeed a little house in which our soul dwells and then, in death we leave the house, lay it to rest, and journey on to God.

Father Reiser's siblings, from left: Alex, Lynn Maciej,
Sr. Bertrand O.S.B., Fr. Reiser, and Rosemary Leger.

When I looked at my brother Alex's still body shortly after his death, it was then that I really cherished and appreciated more deeply what a wonderful gift is the gift of faith; to see beyond the physical and to walk with God in the Kingdom beyond the stars. More than ever before, as I looked at his body, I appreciated and realized more deeply that it was indeed only the shell. The great spirit of Alex had gone to his Creator and he was, at that moment, appreciating the great mysteries of God. He was having unfolded before him the beauty and the glory of the Kingdom. The mystery of faith that we so struggle with, he now embraced, understood and appreciated with absolute clarity. Now he knew all the answers, the riddles of science, the complexities of our theological truths. Now he understood them all in the fullness of God's presence. Alex's death has deepened my faith in how important faith really is. Faith helps one meet the challenge of death, to be moved beyond space and time and to appreciate what is the reality of life beyond death, what it means to leave here and go to God.

My loss of vision at breakfast deepened my appreciation for sight. My brother's death helped me appreciate more keenly how wonderful faith in God really is. ✝

Even a glass of water is a gift

"Taking it for granted" fits many areas of our life quite appropriately. We move on through a day without pausing to appreciate the beautiful conveniences we have and often expect.

All of this was prompted by the dry faucets that greeted me Saturday morning. One of the switches in our well went out of operation and put a big shutoff to that fresh cool water that normally would greet me first thing in the morning. No refreshing shower; no water to shave; no brushing of teeth or cool splattering of water on the face; the hard reality of only one flush left in the toilet.

I thought of those Arabs I saw living in the Egyptian desert who experience quite a hardship getting the H_2O they use and how I just expect this wonderful convenience of life.

Thanks to Jerry Koch, the water is running again and the Rambling Reiser does not have to use excessive portions of cologne to counterbalance the absence of cool, running water. ✝

Clean, safe drinking water isn't a guarantee for the world's poorest citizens. Reiser Relief Inc., delivers water to Haitians six-days-a-week.

Comparisons always lead to discontent

They say the grass is always greener on the other side of the fence. It reminds me of days back on the farm when we would see the cows sticking their heads between the barbed-wire fence to try and get that bit of grass, that to them I'm sure, seemed greener and far more appetizing than that which was on their side of the barbed wire.

We're all a great deal like the cows looking through the fence and seeing the grass on the other side. For many, it seems as if it is always greener in somebody else's yard, or somebody else's life is a little easier or more fulfilling or more delightful than our own. Perhaps they have more of the conveniences and luxuries and pleasures of life than we enjoy and so the old green eye of envy gets a little stronger and brighter by the day.

Something that proves very helpful for me, and helps to raise my spirits, is to see how much better off I am than so many other people. In the course of every day, I see so many people who have trials and tribulations beyond compare, others who have physical handicaps and a host of privations that stare them in the face, day after day. One could list many, many problems and difficulties that others possess and carry, that we do not have to face, and the more we look at them and think about them, the more we realize how fortunate and blessed we are with what we have.

When we add it all together we discover that our cross is not quite as heavy and not quite as big as that which many others carry. We are far more blessed. Then, we begin to realize within our own hearts that we are very lucky to be in the circumstances we are in.

Dissatisfaction causes a lot of problems, anxieties and discomfort. The more we are pleased, content with what we have and where we're at, the more joy and peace and blessings come into our life.

We all indeed could spend a little extra time counting our blessings rather than numbering our crosses. If we were to lay our blessings side by side, we would soon discover that our blessings are far greater in number than our crosses. Then we need lay our crosses alongside of another's crosses and we discover that ours are indeed quite small by comparison.

Try it for one day. Just count your blessings and overlook the crosses and burdens. It will be a better day, a happier day, and certainly there will be a little extra twinkle in your eye when people meet you here and there. †

Adopt an attitude of gratitude

Easter is always a grand and glorious feast. What is greater than to celebrate not only the reality of Christ's resurrection but also the assurance that some day we too shall rise in a magnificent glorified body? What a wonderful joy to have the destiny of sharing the wonders of Heaven in our complete person of soul and body.

We have so much to be thankful for and how seldom we pause during the course of each day to reflect on the many blessings God shares with us.

The above was sparked by the following quotation I received from my friend Tony: "Charles Spurgeon once remarked sadly that God's people write their blessings in the sand, but engrave their troubles in marble."

Contentment and gratitude can be learned. We cannot control our circumstances, but we can control the level of contentment within those circumstances! To help us do that, we could start by keeping a journal in which we write down just one good thing that happens each day or just one thing for which we are grateful during each day. It may be nothing more than "Boy, I'm sure glad today is over." Try it. It is certainly a much more lasting record than writing in sand and it may just be the key to a turning point in your lives. ✝

Gratitude keeps us humble

Sunday, August 9, was one of those hot, muggy days and people knew that it was summer in Minnesota. Everyone was grateful for air conditioning, wherever it was available, and it was a sweet respite from the weather outside. The day was a tremendous contrast to those beautiful cool days of July during which I heard a few complain about the cold weather. I trust that they remembered their thoughts on that hot Sunday.

Contrast is always a blessing. It gives one an opportunity to appreciate a lot of those things we so often take for granted. Hot days give one an opportunity to be grateful for the cool ones. The blessing of a good rain, even on a picnic, is appreciated when you have experienced a real drought.

We all have an abundance of blessings and gifts that are so easily taken for granted and not always sufficiently appreciated.

Some years ago I broke my leg, and the cast, which remained on for three months, gave me much opportunity to say, "Thank you, Lord," for the ability to walk. The break was nearly fifteen years ago, yet every time I'm obliged to walk an extra block or so because of parking, I think of how good it is to walk freely without crutches, even if it is an extra block.

A couple of weeks ago I had cataract surgery on my right eye, and the time that it was bandaged gave me a beautiful opportunity to appreciate a little more keenly what eyesight is all about.

We all fail, in some extent, in showing sufficient appreciation to Almighty God for the wonderful things He gives us day after day; things for which He doesn't charge us but just says: "Here they are. I give them to you because I love you."

How we need to pause frequently throughout the day and say, "Thanks, Lord, it has been good of you to be so kind and generous."

Gratitude also helps to keep us a little more humble, for we realize that these great treasures of life are God's gift and not a matter of our own doing.

We expect children to say "thank you" for a little two-cent lollipop. How much more do we need to say "thank you" to a God who is so absolutely magnificent and wonderful to each one of us. Yes, thanks, Lord, for everything. ✝

The Fatima Shrine at Epiphany Church.

Take note of the special
people in your lives

Last Sunday's homily about the stained glass windows in our church revealed some obvious facts, one of which is that we all take many things for granted and until they are pointed out to us, we remain rather oblivious.

In all five Masses, there was no one who could name the theme of each of the six large windows in the main body of the church. Some have been coming into that space for ten-and-a-half years but never really focused on what the windows were all about. They were just taken for granted. Now that it has been mentioned, I would wager that next Sunday everyone will be taking an extra peak at them and striving to keep in memory what the theme is of each of them.

The same reality is true in so many, many facets of life. We take so many things for granted and then some day that reality is gone and we grieve over our past lack of attention. How true this is of so many people in our lives that we share with, work with or live with. We never really ever give them any real personal expression of appreciation or gratitude until it is too late. It is the old question of "a dime short and a day late."

How important it is that someone wakes us up and makes us more attuned to some of the wonderful people in our lives that we overlook and take for granted. The first group are all of the people near us, how we need to be more responsive, more appreciative, more grateful for them and tell them how much they mean to us, how important and how valuable they are in our daily lives and not wait until they are in a casket, no longer hearing what we are saying. We need to do today what we have put off for far too long a time and not procrastinate until tomorrow. Tell the person this very day how much they really mean to us.

There is also another reality that we so take for granted —

God's gifts, His bounteousness, and the many blessings that He continually showers upon us without interruption. Life and all of the wonderful realities that surround it are God's personal expression of love, caring and concern for us. How often we fail to express our gratitude to say, just a quick little, "Thank you, Lord; it's been wonderful."

The parable of the ten lepers and how only one came back to say thank you always annoyed me. I felt a little personal resentment against the other nine; that is, until I was wise enough to pray and ponder how I perhaps am one of those nine in my failure to really express gratitude to the Lord, who gives so much, hears so often, heals so frequently, forgives without reservation and still showers my life with an abundance of blessings that I could surely not enumerate.

I'm sure everyone will notice the windows a little more attentively in the months ahead, but how far more important it is to notice those people who are special in our lives, and to say: "Thank you. I love you. You've done a great job. You are really special."

It will make their day, and your day, so much better. We all need to do it today. ✝

Home should be a refuge
from the world's negative influences

It was about 9:15 in the morning and there was a gentle rain falling when I was driving behind our senior housing complex. There, before me, was a mother duck with about ten or twelve little ducklings. As the mother duck made her way through the bright green grass, the little ones were crowded close to her for the safety and security she offered to them. It was a heartwarming scene and I felt like going over and picking up one of the little ones and holding it in the palm of my hand; but that would have been a foolish endeavor for they would have scampered away before I got anywhere close.

Nature has so many delightful and beautiful scenes. They are such a wonderful contrast to the brick, tar and concrete of our modem civilization and how important it is to stop long enough to smell the roses and see the wonders, which God has so lavishly surrounded us.

The duck family reminded me of our human families and how we need to maintain a good togetherness, a mutual support, one for another. Within our homes there needs to be much love, lots of kindness, overflowing buckets of patience, ready forgiveness and a sacrificial spirit that places the needs of the other members prior to one's own.

The world is full of so much violence and turmoil. There is so much kicking, shoving and striving to get to the top that we need a place where we can come to and have a refuge from all those things we encounter in the world. We need to find a haven of peace in our home where we can expect and receive tenderness, devotion, comfort and peace.

Our first thought should not be what the other family members should do, but first say to ourselves: "What can I do to create a peaceful and loving atmosphere in our home?" If each asked themselves the question and then followed through and did the positive, then there would be a new haven of refuge within our households.

Quarreling, fighting, contention, yelling, screaming, shouting and caustic remarks do only one thing — they destroy the very structure of a family.

After you've read this Rambling, pass it on to the other members of the family and then sit down and have a little roundtable discussion. Share ideas as to how you can make your family home a better, more loving, joyous place to live. Everyone needs to have input, everyone needs to be involved so they feel part of the action and part of the building process to have our home the way the Lord wishes it to be.

My thanks to the lovely mother duck and all those fluffy little ducklings for prompting these ideas and reflections. If I hadn't seen them, this Rambling would never have come about. Isn't it wonderful how God can touch our hearts and move our spirits? †

A great diversity of people
makes up this wonderful country

Over the years since the Pilgrims first came to this land, the shores of our country have been open to a great variety of peoples. The oppressed, the victimized, the ostracized, the persecuted, the needy, the homeless, those who for one reason or another found a need to leave their own land, came to a country with apparent endless resources and unending opportunities and ever expanding frontiers.

Perhaps, many have felt the policy too open and too broad over the 200 years of our existence. If there are negatives to the issue, I am not debating them but rather seeing the host of positives that speak loud and strong.

We have gathered a rich inheritance of many cultures and nationalities and assembled them into a coat of many vibrant colors! Each country rich in traditions that reach deeply into the lifestyle of their people became our blessing as the people came ashore. There were Swedes, Norwegians, Germans, Poles, English, Irish, Spaniards, Italians, Greeks, Jews, Portuguese, French, Russians, Slavics, Dutch, Belgians, Asians, Mexicans, Central and South Americans, and others too numerous to mention. They came in their own uniqueness and specialness and each has enriched our country beyond measure.

The "open arms" policy has brought an abundance and diversity of culture to our country. So, also, as we open our hearts and hands to all around us, we are enriched in a similar manner. †

We each manifest God's creativity

Uncle Henry was my Godmother's husband and a very opinionated individual. He said what was on his mind and his convictions were rather firm. I shall never forget the day he remarked to me: "Thanks be to God we're all different; for if it weren't that way, everyone would have wanted to marry my wife and then we would have been in a mess of trouble."

Everyone is different; everyone is unique. We each have our own likes and dislikes and our own particular philosophies and approaches to life. We need to respect other persons' views and convictions and they need be willing to respect ours.

Tolerance is a great quality of life and how we need to exercise it day by day. Just because someone disagrees with us does not mean they are wrong, let alone bad; but it means that they have a contrary perception to what we have.

The little pansy is quite different and distinct from the big blossom of the mum; the little white birch is a sliver in comparison to the giant redwood of California. Each element of nature is different and each manifests God in its own particular way, and so it is with humans. Each of us is a different person, a unique individual and we each manifest God's creativeness in a very special manner.

One of my good friends of fifty years is someone with whom I often disagree with very strongly. As I look back over five decades of friendship, I can never remember that we were ever angry with each other or raised our voices in a quarrel because we respect each other's right to his particular view.

My former Pastor, Fr. Nick Finn, with whom I worked for fifteen years at St. Mary of the Lake in White Bear Lake, had a marvelous saying that I often think of. It went as follows: "It's a great Church that holds us all."

Isn't that a marvelous saying? It's one that says the Lord's arms are open for all. Jesus embraces each and every one of us, regardless of our diversities, loves us with an infinite love and wants us to walk with Him down life's pathways. If God is that open and loving to each of us, we too must show a great measure of tolerance for the differences that we discover in others. Whether it's a pansy or a mum, a birch or a redwood, an apple or a pear, a chicken or a duck, differences aren't very significant for each reflects God in a unique way.

May each of us, as humans, be happy with being the unique and special individual God made us. Everyone is made to a special blueprint in the mind of God, and as the old saying goes, "God doesn't make junk."

So, you be you and I'll be me and let's really realize that God made us both. †

Fr. Reiser transfered to St. Paul Seminary in 1944 after attending
St. John's University in Collegeville, Minnesota. He once wrote
that he considered monastic life for a while, but it became
clear to him that Diocesan Priesthood was his calling.
He was ordained on June 4, 1949, by Archbishop
John Gregory Murray. His first Solemn Mass was at
Holy Name of Jesus, the parish he attended as a child.
Fr. Reiser is pictured in the fourth row
from the top in the fifth photo from the left.

SECTION FIVE

God's Grace At Work Within Us

God's Grace At Work Within Us

My family's farm was on the edge of a small lake. The water was surrounded by woods except for our shoreline. In a north bay, closest to the farm, was an island with a cluster of trees whose roots were no doubt nourished by the water that surrounded them. This island was a favorite place of mine when I was a boy; I would go and sit in the shadow of the trees looking at water all around.

One spring the rains came in abundance and continued into the summer. Soon, the ground around the trees was covered with water until at last the trees stood immersed in the lake. Slowly but surely, the trees died, overpowered by the same water that once nourished their roots. The island eventually disappeared and the trees, lifeless, fell and soon floated away.

When I think of the lake, the lovely island and the beautiful trees, I am reminded of the spiritual life of so many. People are like the trees growing beautifully on the island and the water surrounding the island are the things of the world, namely the materialistic and secular influences of our modern society. As the number of material things and worldly interests increase, like the water, they slowly sap the individual of their spiritual life and growth.

Matters of God become less and less important as our interest in secular matters increase. When we focus on the pocketbook and material resources, which we rely upon to pay for worldly desires and various entertainments, our dependence on God is lessened. Soon, prayer loses its value; reliance on a fat checkbook takes the place of a Providential God. The life of the spirit becomes less and less important and slowly it is drained from the person's soul. What can be seen, touched, felt and enjoyed overpowers the unseen and the realities of a future life. The glory and joy of the Kingdom, which God has promised to the faithful, are no longer taken seriously. How quickly the things of the world can wash away the storehouse of the spiritual that has been built over previous years.

We all live on the island of the spirit and we are surrounded by the worldly attractions that oftentimes seem so appealing, so delightful and so much to be sought after. But, like the water surrounding the island, they slowly gain greater hold, greater power, over the spiritual trees in our life.

I urge everyone to take inventory on how worldly things are encroaching on their spiritual life. Are we losing our grip on the great principles and teachings of Christ that we gained in our younger years? Are matters of God slowly getting watered down, rendered less and less important?

It is good to regularly take inventory of where we are in our relationship to God and the spiritual state of our soul. Is our island of the spirit growing stronger and expanding, or is the "water" of the world encroaching upon our spiritual fortifications? Youth, middle-aged or senior, it is never too early to take inventory of your spiritual life and to evaluate where you are in your journey to Heaven.

Don't wait until your spiritual island has been washed away by the waters of a worldly existence. Jesus once said: *What profit does a man show who gains the whole world and destroys himself in the process.* (Mark 8:36)

These Ramblings offer considerations as you fortify yourself against the worldly influences that could otherwise engulf you. †

Conversion means
changing for the better

Fall is a wonderful time of the year. There is so much color, beauty and splendor wherever you look. It is this wonderful season that makes Minnesota a great and glorious place to live. One can look forward to this grand time and experience the wide range of fall colors, the beautiful reds, oranges, yellows and all of the colors in between. The maples seem to strive to outdo one another in their exquisite color and beauty.

I saw a maple the other day so perfectly formed and its color was absolutely lavish. You would think that each particular leaf had been especially and individually painted by a great artist, and of course, that artist is Almighty God.

The trees, in all of their colorful splendor, are a sharp contrast to the ordinary greens of summer.

In a certain respect, we are spiritually like those maple trees going from green to the very colorful foliage of fall. Each of us, in our own particular way, has a spiritual need for conversion, for a change of life in one way or the other. We have faults and failings. We have habits that are not the very best. There always is the need to change, to have a conversion of heart, a newness of spirit.

On occasion there are radical conversions such as were experienced by Saul of Tarsus who became the great Evangelist Paul, Mary Magdalene who became the faithful follower of Jesus, the Apostles (all but John) who were afraid to be at the cross of Christ but later, without hesitation, laid down their lives in heroic acts of martyrdom.

For most, conversions are of a smaller and lesser degree. It means improving our spiritual life, our relationship with God. Conversion means change, change from something not so good to something better or from average to better or best.

God is very sensitive to these conversions of heart and when they occur He adorns our soul with the beauties and the glories that only God can bestow and which will be so very evident as we enter the Kingdom of Heaven. Saint Paul in one of his letters, says: *One is the glory of the Son, another the glory of the moon, and another the glory of the stars, for star differeth from star in glory. So also is the resurrection of the dead.* (1 Corinthians 15:41)

God will reward each individual person for those particular efforts that they have expended as they walk the path of life. We shall be blessed according to our labors.

Conversion of life is for each of us. It means changing some of our ways that are not so good to those which are better and to take good habits and refine them into something that is even more pleasing to God. There is always room for improvement, always opportunity to change for the better, because our model is Jesus Christ, the Son of God.

We all have the opportunity of changing the spiritually green color of our lives into the radiant beauties and colors of the Lord. We do it for God's glory and for our own future enrichment in the Kingdom. †

Our Lord deserves our reverence

I always love to read the story about Moses at the burning bush and how God spoke to him as follows:

There an angel of the Lord appeared to him in fire flaming out of a bush. As he looked on, he was surprised to see that the bush, though on fire, was not consumed. So Moses decided to go over to look at this remarkable sight, and see why the bush is not burned.

When the Lord saw him coming over to look at it more closely, God called out to him from the bush. "Moses! Moses!" He answered, "Here I am." God said, "Come no nearer! Remove the sandals from your feet, for the place where you stand is holy ground. I am the God Lord of your father," He continued, "the God of Jacob." Moses hid his face, for he was afraid to look at God. (Exodus 3:2-6)

The great leader of the Jewish people was reminded of the reverence we as creatures owe our great God. We need to be reminded that we are creatures and He is the Eternal, the Almighty Lord of Heaven and Earth.

We live in an age in which so little is held reverent, so much is held so commonplace and ordinary. Like so many things, mystery has kind of gotten lost in the shuffle.

The above was generated by my reflection on the movie, *The Last Temptation of Christ*. It appears they wish to reduce our great God and Savior Jesus Christ to the ordinary and to the commonplace. What a tragedy it is when humans use their God-given gifts to insult the one who so generously gave them the various talents they possess.

There's a wonderful section in the Book of Job that is worthy of our consideration. It is God speaking to Job:

I will question you and you tell me the answers! Where were you when I founded the earth? Tell me, if you have understanding. Who determined its size; do you know? Who stretched out the measuring line for it? Into what were its pedestals sunk, and who laid the cornerstone, while the morning stars sang in chorus and all the sons of God shouted for joy? And who shut within doors the sea, when it burst forth from the womb; when I made the clouds its garment and thick darkness its swaddling bands? When I set limits for it and fastened the bar of its door, and said, "Thus far shall you come but no farther, and here shall your proud waves be stilled!" Have you ever in your lifetime commanded the morning and shown the dawn its place? (Job 38:3-12)

Directors like Martin Scorsese come and go, and they pollute and contaminate with their irreverence and insensitivity that which is sacred and holy to those who believe.

Despite the dark clouds, there have been some bright rays of sunshine from it all. Whenever a loved one is attacked, those who really love and care deepen their own love and devotion to the one attacked. May our own love and devotion to the Lord Jesus be enriched during these days when others may abuse Him. ✝

Hope is found in the promise of God

What is one of the greatest support forces in all the world?
It sustains us when times are difficult and nearly unbearable.
It brings strength when all other supports seem to fail and are

Mark Sanislo

The late Pope John Paul II was a hero to Fr. Reiser,
personifying the hope that can be found in Christ Jesus.

ineffective. It is available to kings as well as paupers, to the Ph.D. as well as the child in first grade. Corporate chair people have reliance upon it and manual laborers have confidence in it. It is a support to Popes and presidents, as well as to Little Leaguers. Have you guessed what it is? It is the virtue of hope that is based on God. The virtue of hope has its foundation in the promises of Jesus Christ.

The world we know is passing away; all things of time and matter have a timeline on them, a timeline that has an eventual ending. Paul said to the Corinthians: *The world in its present form is passing away.* (1 Corinthians 7:31)

The wise person places his security and trust in the word of Jesus. How quickly we can lose our material goods in any number of tragedies or disasters. Sickness, injury, or the death of a loved one, quickly preaches a great message of the unimportance of the things of this world. We need to have our heart set on the eternal rewards of Heaven.

The people we saw in Haiti have very little to hope for in this life, and tomorrow has only the bleak and stark reality of another day that is overflowing with privations. They can rely only on the promises of Christ that give an assurance of an eternity filled with the blessings of a Heaven where joy and happiness are far beyond the human imagination.

Each of us experience trials and tribulations in different ways, but each has the great opportunity to rely on the same hope that Jesus gives us. We all have our little and greater crucifixions, but we need to always remember the Easter Sunday that follows.

Lent is a wonderful time to renew our hope and trust in a God that assures us of greater things to come.

His promises never fail, for He loves each of us with the same infinite love; for He has created us to His own image.

Cast your hope on Him and know that it will eventually be fulfilled. ✝

Marian devotion leads to the Eucharist

The journey to Fatima in Portugal and to Lourdes in France was an extraordinary prayerful experience. These two Marian shrines provide an awesome atmosphere in which one communicates and shares with God in a very easy and peaceful manner.

At Fatima, Mary appeared to three peasant children and at Lourdes, she appeared to Bernadette. It was at Lourdes that Mary proclaimed that she was the Immaculate Conception; that she was conceived without sin.

Mary's admonitions at all of her apparitions, no matter where they occurred throughout the world, were always telling us to follow the Gospel — the teachings of Jesus Christ. Her continuing message is one of increased prayer, deeper penance, more frequent reception of the Sacraments of Confession and Holy Communion, and a life of greater self-discipline. Mary's messages are not a revelation of things that are new, but a continual prodding to do what Jesus asked us to do 2,000 years ago.

Mary looks at all of us as her children, for it was on the Cross that Jesus entrusted all people to the loving care of His Mother and He admonished all to respect her as their Spiritual Mother. Mothers are always looking out for the well-being of their children, seeking what is best for them. We cannot expect anything less from our Spiritual Mother in Heaven, Mary the Mother of Jesus.

The candlelight procession at Lourdes is absolutely overpowering. To experience 20,000 people carrying candles, saying the Hail Mary, and singing the Lourdes Hymn, would touch even the hardest heart. People from many, many countries, each saying the Rosary in their own particular language, all of them God's children asking the Mother of the Son of God to intercede for them.

In our seminary training there was a Latin phrase we often heard, *Ad Jesum Per Mariam*, meaning, "To Jesus through Mary." What a wonderful reality that is. It was Mary who interceded with her Son for the couple celebrating their wedding at Cana, and the Lord worked His first miracle. She gave to God Himself, flesh and blood. What power of intercession she indeed possesses. She does not grant our petitions on her own, but humbly submits them to her Divine Son.

True Marian devotion leads to the Eucharist, for he who loves the Mother cannot help but love the Son, and vice versa. That is why, at all the various Marian Shrines that I have visited, in a great number of countries, there is always a great devotion to the Mass and the receiving of Holy Communion. For it is Mary's role to present her Son to us and to bring us to His feet.

Mary's great prayer is, of course, the Rosary, the wonderful unfolding of the life of Jesus. Being Christian means to follow Christ and what better way to follow him than to meditate on the varying scenes of His lifetime. The Rosary, before or after Mass, is indeed most appropriate, for Mary was on Calvary's Hill, offering her Son to God the Father on our behalf. At the Mass, which is the sacrifice of Calvary renewed in unbloody manner, we join with Mary at the foot of the Cross, and offer the Lord Jesus to God the Father in praise of His glory, in thanksgiving for His blessings, in petition for pardon, and as individuals asking for many blessings.

Yes, the one who holds the hand of Mary cannot help but hold the hand of Christ, and walk with Him to the glory of the Father in Heaven. †

Jesus learned about the world from His mother

She was a gentle, patient, quiet, loving woman. She guided me during my first twenty-four years of life. She was soft-spoken, and never prone to anger or sarcasm. She preached powerfully by her style of life and the Christian atmosphere that seemed to continually surround her. Her words of wisdom flowed gracefully from her heart in a simple and powerful fashion. They would be long remembered by the thin little fellow that walked often at her side.

One such pearl of great price was spoken to me when I was about ten years of age and we were picking raspberries in the patch to the west of the house. We were facing each other, she on the north side of the row and I on the south and she shared the following words of advice, "Bernie, don't ever be afraid to die. What you are getting is so much better than what you've got."

I watched her leave this earth some eighteen years later and it was as peaceful as a child going to sleep. Her last breath was peaceful and gentle and the words she had spoken years before came to my memory: *Don't be afraid to die. What you are getting is so much better than what you've got.*

By now, I'm sure you know that I am speaking of the woman I called "Ma," a short two-lettered word that identified the one who was the very heart and soul of our family circle and life. Her name was Ottilia.

Sunday Mass, the Sacraments, family prayer were as natural as eating three farm meals a day. They were just part of life. Walking a mile to church in three feet of snow against the north wind was not considered extraordinary; it was just what you needed to do. The Lord was a real part of our life and Sunday was His day, come what may, neither sleet nor snow, mud nor rain hindered us going to Church on Sunday morning, to thank God for all we had received during the week.

Fr. Reiser's mother, Ottilia, passed away in 1954,
just five years after his ordination to the priesthood.

There was another mother-son relationship that was very inspiring to me and that was the one that took place in Nazareth. The woman's name was Mary and the son was Jesus. There it was that the Blessed Lady fashioned and formed the human qualities and virtues of the one that came down from Heaven and was to walk the roads of Galilee, climb Calvary's hill and be glorified in a magnificent Resurrection on Easter. The distinct mannerisms, His inflections of speech and so on, Jesus learned from His mother, Mary, as they lived out their life in the humble place of Nazareth. What a powerful influence she had on Him from birth to death, and when she stood at the foot of the Cross, He said to all of us: *Behold your mother.* (John 19:26-27)

She had touched and influenced His life in many wonderful ways and I wonder how many of His human characteristics can be directly referred back to the woman called Mother Mary.

These are just some of the thoughts that race through my heart and mind as we proceed in building our shrine in honor of the Blessed Lady of Fatima. I know her Son, Jesus, will be very pleased with the devotion and honor we show His mother because no one loved her as much as He loved her, and when we love her, we certainly strike a chord within His heart.

Each of you has your own thoughts to share. The previous are just some of mine and they will be foremost in my heart and mind as I make my way through the shrine when it is completed. We want it to be a place of prayer and reflection for all God's children. May it offer you a place of refuge where you can walk the paths, pause at the various holy areas of the stations, the rosary, the Fatima scene, the Pieta, the Risen Christ, and ponder what all of these mean in your life and in the life to come.

I must admit this is one of the more exciting times of my life as I see the Shrine unfold, and I recall some words Archbishop John Roach said to me years ago when I was beginning another project. He merely said, "Bernie, give it your best shot." And so I shall. †

Fr. Reiser visits the Fatima Shrine
on the Epiphany Church campus. Fr. Reiser has
a special devotion to the Blessed Virgin Mary.

The real struggles of the world are struggles of the spirit

The Spirit was "a moving all over this place." How true those words were as Bishop Welsh shared the powerful sacrament of Confirmation with our young people. It was a time of high emotions, and the liturgy was sparked by the elegant choir with so many magnificent refrains, by the stirring brass and timpani that always puts a tingle down your back, the bell choir with sounds of beauty and David Mertesdorf, directing the entire group with excellence. The ministers at the altar did their task with precision, as did the ushers, lectors and Eucharistic Ministers. Josie Bertie and Mary May had the Church looking really sharp. Bill Klein had prepared his students beautifully. Bishop Welsh was his usual charming, beautiful self. He has such a winning personality and so endears himself to all those he comes in contact with. The center of all of the action was, of course, those to be confirmed. They had prepared well over the past several years and this preparation was brought to a magnificent completion at their weekend retreats.

Confirmation is Pentecost repeated. It is the outpouring of the Holy Spirit, the Third Person of the Blessed Trinity, coming down in all of His glory and power to strengthen those confirmed. At Confirmation, we put on the armor of Christ to resist the materialistic and secular elements of society to clash head on with the devil and the forces of evil. The devil is no imaginary opponent, but as Scripture says, he goes throughout the world as a roaring lion seeking whom he may devour. Those confirmed received not only the Holy Spirit, but the seven gifts of the Holy Spirit: wisdom, understanding, knowledge, counsel, fortitude, piety, and fear of the Lord. They are special powers that God gives us to do a more fitting battle with the devil and his legions.

The real struggles of the world are the struggles of the spirit, for as we win or lose the battle of the spirit so also will we spend eternity in absolute ecstasy or in horrible misery.

The opportunity for God's grace and power is equally open to all people. The degree of its outpouring is determined individually by each of us. Some become saints and others do not; it all depends on the individual's cooperation or response to God's invitation to come and walk with Him. God puts us all on the same starting line and says, "Go for it." What happens from there is our determination. The degree of our asking, the degree of our receptivity to God's graces and blessings determines our union with Him.

I like to imagine that God takes us out to a great airport and there before us we see a whole fleet of jet airplanes of different size and speed, and He lets us make the choice as to which we want to fly, how high and how fast. The fuel is God's Grace, the throttle is in our hands and it is our free will that determines how much of that Grace of God, His divine life, will be fed into our lives to make us soar like eagles to the very heights of Heaven. Every day is an exciting day in our spiritual campaign of life.

My prayer for the newly confirmed is that they will really cooperate with the Holy Spirit that was given to them, that He will be a vibrant part of their daily lives and that they will give Him the green light to really work and operate within their lives. The handle on the door to God is on our side, and it is for us to open that door, to invite Him in, and from there on great things happen. ✝

There is joy in Heaven
when we turn from sin

Enthusiasm plus! That would be saying it mildly as we watched the Twins pound the Cards into the ground in the first two games of the World Series.

I pen these Ramblings on Sunday evening October 18, 1987. Today's Minneapolis *Star Tribune* said the crowd's roar after Dan Gladden's grand slam registered 118 decibels — about the same level generated by a jet taking off. There were 55,000 vigorous sets of vocal cords giving it all they had to spur on the glorious Minnesota Twins. My-oh-my, it was a great party and how beautifully everyone got into the act.

A few statistics on the first game's sales were: 25,000 sweatshirts, 5,000 bags of pretzels, 8,000 gallons of beer, 6,000 gallons of pop, 30,000 brats and hot dogs, and 5,000 boxes of popcorn.

No doubt about it, 55,000 strong Minnesotans can let the world know how they feel about the team that has brought fame and glory to the Gopher State.

It all made me think of how much enthusiasm there must be in Heaven when a sinner leaves the ways of wrong-doing and turns back to God. Jesus once said: *I tell you there will likewise be more joy in Heaven over one repentant sinner than over ninety-nine righteous people who have no need to repent.* (Luke 15:7)

Can you imagine billions and billions of Saints and Angels whooping it up when God scores another victory over the devil, when a sinner moves back to God's circle? Those cheers are for the real trophy that lasts forever in the Kingdom of God.

If we think there is excitement at the Dome, we haven't seen anything until we see the real action in the life beyond the stars. So keep on giving the Lord all you've got; the benefits will exceed your greatest expectations or dreams.

Thanks for the inspiration, Twins. Let's take the Cards in five! ✝

He will shield
you from suffering

One of the most paralyzing forces that can grip the human person is fear, and the varieties of fear are nearly an endless list. Fear is torturing and renders so many powers, talents and opportunities of an individual unused or unfulfilled. The following excerpt from St. Francis de Sales is worth reading:

Do not look forward to the trials and crosses of this life with dread or fear. Rather, look to them with full confidence that, as they arise, God to Whom you belong will deliver you from them.

He has guided and guarded you this far in life. Do you but hold fast to His dear Hand, and He will lead you safely through all trials.

Whenever you cannot stand, He will carry you lovingly in His arms.

Do not look forward to what may happen tomorrow. The same Eternal Father who cares for you today will take good care of you tomorrow, and every day of your life. Either He will shield you from suffering or He will give you the unfailing strength to bear it.

Be at peace, then, and put aside all useless thoughts, all vain dreads, and all anxious imaginations. ✝

Share in the wonder of Heaven

Fall is always a beautiful time of the year, The crispness in the morning and the evening air, the flocks of geese hovering overhead in their beautiful wedge-shaped formations getting ready for their trip to the south, the hardy flowers holding on after a few light touches of frost, the grass seems greener and the lakes seem to have magic in their waves and turbulence.

Something more exciting, thrilling and delightful than the above is the splendid colors of fall. The golden colors are as radiant and sparkling as newly-plated vessels of gold. The maple trees seem to vie with one another as to which manifests the greatest splash of color, whether it is varying shades of red, orange or yellow, God, the Great Artist, does a magnificent job painting the bright colors over His handiwork of creation.

As God looks at His creation, He certainly sees the reflection of His beauty here, there and everywhere. Beauty that is only a shadow of the beauty that He Himself possesses, and a beauty that we shall behold forever in the Kingdom of Heaven.

The transformation of a Minnesota landscape in the fall is a delight to any eye, but there is another transformation that we can not see that is more radiant, elegant, magnificent and glorious than the most wonderful maple clothed in the colors of fall. I speak of the beauty of the soul that is filled with God's grace, God's life, where God sees the very image of Himself, a soul that is a temple for His Presence. The Bible says: *You must know that your body is a temple of the Holy Spirit.* (1 Corinthians 6:19)

Those who walk with God and live with Him are indeed sharers in the wonders of Heaven. When the sinner turns away from his evil ways and has a conversion of heart and soul, God touches his soul with the wonderful wand of beauty and he becomes radiant with God's very own life.

Those who walk with God and refresh their soul with frequent

Holy Communion, prayer, penance, and good works, are continu-ally enhancing the beauty of their soul with a greater sharing in God's life which is the very source of all beauty.

As you watch the beauties of fall unfold in all of their radiant colors, may it be a little time to reflect on the beauty of your soul, and to evaluate how close you walk with God. Is the Lord a con-tinuing companion of yours as you walk the path of life?

The beautiful leaves of autumn will eventually fall and be cov-ered with ice and snow, but the beauty of the soul shall go on for-ever, unless the individual turns away from God. May we always be conscious of the beauty that dwells within us and preserve it with great determination, and strive to enhance it with the passing of each day. †

There is but one breath
between us and eternity

Can you imagine putting all of your earthly possessions together and then flipping a coin for double or nothing? Most would say that anyone doing that would be in need of some psychiatric help. It would be a terribly big gamble and not one in harmony with good reasoning.

On the other hand something greater than all our possessions rides on every second of our earthly journey and that is eternal life — being in Heaven or Hell for all eternity.

My friend, Tony, shared a penetrating thought with me the other day at lunch, as we enjoyed pancakes, fried eggs and sausage. "There is only one breath between myself and eternity, and I don't know which breath it will be."

Give that some sober and quiet thought. How quickly life here on Earth can end and how frequently it happens to friends and relatives. We always kind of think it will be someone else.

I never know when that last breath will be but the state of my soul, when it comes, will set the stage for my dwelling place forever. Too frequently we get so caught up with the business of this world's activities that we lose sight of what is the most important part of life, our eternal life.

We need to take a few moments each day to see how we are doing on the spiritual ledger of life. Is it getting the attention that it should? A flip of the coin often decides much in life's endeavors but a single breath decides far more. †

Only the eternal is important

Above the triple doorways of Milan Cathedral there are three inscriptions.

Over one door is carved a beautiful wreath of roses and underneath is the legend: *All that which pleases is but for a moment.*

Over another is sculptured a cross with the words: *All that which troubles is but for a moment.*

But over the central entrance to the main aisle is the inscription: *That only is important which is eternal.*

We all need basic principles to guide us down the pathways of life, and if we have them it is relatively easy to make prudent judgments and wise decisions in the varying moments of life.

All of the pleasures of life are but for the moment in comparison to the endless expanses of eternity, where the soul is filled with perfect joy and embraces, with all of its individual human potential, the beauty of God.

As we encounter the varying troubles, crosses and afflictions of life, they too are but for the moment in comparison to that endless expanse of eternity that God enfolds before us as we leave Mother Earth and pass on to the Kingdom of Heaven.

The above principles are a powerful reminder to us that when we experience the various pleasures and excitement of this life, they are of very short duration and nothing in comparison to what God has prepared for us in the next life. We should not hold on too strongly to this earth's pleasures, but rather leave them be a reminder of the magnificent and wonderful experience of joy God will give us in the next.

Also, when we encounter suffering, hardship and trial, we need to sustain them with a deep faith, an unending hope and assurance that they will someday cease when come the blessings that will more than compensate for what we may have endured in our day to day experiences. We need to keep before us the words over the central entrance to the Milan Cathedral: *That only is important which is eternal.*

Inscribe that short sentence into your heart and refer to it often, as you move through the paces of each day. †

Breaking ground for an Epiphany
building project started in April 1966.

We should work
for the retirement that never ends

How big is the ocean? That's a rather broad question, but when we flew over to Australia, I certainly became aware of how large it really is. We left Los Angeles on a Northwest airliner and flew 14 hours and 40 minutes for a total of 7,498 miles before we reached Sydney. That's a lot of water to cover, to say the least, and then to consider how deep the ocean is, blows your mind as to the number of gallons that an ocean contains. At its deepest point, the Pacific Ocean is 36,198 feet below sea level.

How long would it take to fill the ocean at the rate of one drop at a time?

When I was a youngster in grade school, one of the Sisters told the little story about the Saint who asked: "How long is eternity?"

"If an Angel came and took one drop of water out of the ocean every thousand years," the Sister recounted, "when the ocean was bone dry, then God might say 'eternity is just beginning.'"

Yes, eternity has no end but it's hard for the human mind to conceive the reality that there is no conclusion, no termination, never a final Amen.

As we walk the pathways of life, we need to frequently meditate on some of the fundamental spiritual realities. One is that our life here on earth is so very, very short. What are a hundred years, and how few live that long, in comparison to an eternity that never ends? We need to often lay our trials, tribulations, sufferings, pains and all of the heartache of life alongside of the reality of what lies in store for us in the Kingdom beyond death.

How hard and long people work for a retirement that oftentimes is so very, very short. We should work, then, for the retirement that never ends. We get so enmeshed in the things of the world and we lose sight of what are the big things that really count. As Scripture says: *What does it profit a man to gain the whole world and suffer the loss of his soul?* (Mark 8:36)

Religion, leading a good life, doing what God wants us to do, are really the only things that make sense when you reflect and consider what eternity really means. Our destiny is eternal joy or eternal misery, Heaven or Hell forever.

So this is just one of my little reflections on the journey to Australia. There will be more to come when the spirit moves me. The ocean trip was long, but it was worthwhile, for if it even provoked one good thought that will assist us on our journey to the Kingdom, it has great benefit.

Visualize the Angel coming down and picking up one drop every thousand years from the Pacific Ocean. How long will it really take to empty the ocean? †

Run so as to win

You know that while all the runners in the stadium take part in the race, the award goes to one man. In that case, run so as to win! Athletes deny themselves all sorts of things. They do this to win a crown of leaves that withers, but we a crown that is imperishable! (1 Corinthians 9:4-25)

With all of the press, plus the television and radio coverage this past couple weeks on who the new head coach of the Minnesota Gophers would be, I thought of St. Paul's great words to the people of Corinth over 1,900 years ago.

Things haven't changed much over the centuries, and humans have pretty much the same struggles now as they did then. St. Paul was not only a great preacher and writer but also a great competitor. He was familiar with what was going on around him in his world of the first century. The Greeks were great athletes and the sports games of those early centuries got lots of attention. Winning then, as now, was a big factor in the athletes' daily life and no small concern of the spectator; I'm sure if Paul was around for the games, he was plenty vocal in cheering on his favorite runner.

In fact, in the message to the Corinthians, he says: *Run so as to win*. So, hiring coaches to lead a team to victory is really what the bottom line is all about. St. Paul then comes in with his marvelous challenge to give your spiritual crown of victory the same enthusiasm, spirit, effort and drive.

We would all be looking pretty sharp religiously if the matters of the spirit received as much attention as all these other items to crowd our daily lives.

Yes, the Gophers have a new coach on whom they are placing high hopes for winning many games. We, in turn, have a great Coach who is interested in our achieving one great victory, the Kingdom of Heaven. And the Coach is none other than one called Jesus Christ. Listen to Him. He has a great game plan for each of us. ✝

Not even God can change the past

"One day at a time, sweet Jesus, one day at a time," are the inspirational words of a very touching hymn. It expresses a truth that all of us should hearken to and live as we go through our daily lives.

Jesus Himself said: *Enough, then, of worrying about tomorrow. Let tomorrow take care of itself. Today has troubles enough of its own.* (Matthew 6:34)

He said we need to take one day at a time and not be anticipating the future with our worries or lamenting the past.

The past is gone forever; we can not change it; not even God can change it. We need to bring conclusion to yesterday's concerns and move on. The past is a sack of sand burdening our thoughts of today and hindering us from forward progress. I cannot change yesterday, so why should I keep beating myself to death about it, or allowing it to take the splendor and joy out of the day that I have at hand. I need repent over my mistakes and sins of yesterday, ask God's forgiveness, and then carry on in what a beautiful fashion as done by Paul, Mary Magdalene and the great Peter himself. The wonderful achievements of each of them would never have been, had they sat around with their crying towels, lamenting their past faults, not moving off the square.

There is also the great question of tomorrow. How many people live with the black clouds of fear and anxiety over what might happen tomorrow? The truth of the matter is, I shall never live tomorrow, I only can live today, and I trust in God that He will give me the strength, the power and the grace to deal with the problems and difficulties of today. Jesus assured St. Paul in marvelous fashion: *My grace is sufficient for thee.* (2 Corinthians 12:9)

Those words were spoken by the Lord when Paul was lamenting the thorn in the flesh that was besieging and tormenting him and he asked God to lift it from him. The Lord in plain language said, "Paul, quit crying in your soup, get with the program, and I will take care of you. Just do your best, put your shoulder to the wheel, pray for My help and enjoy the day."

One day not long ago, I asked someone how they were and the response was, "Well, some days aren't as bad as others." My thoughts were, "You don't need a facial lift but an attitude lift."

When Frank and Luella Rudolph were confined to their home and unable get to church any longer because of illness, I went to their home each Tuesday morning for Holy Communion. I would always greet Frank with the words, "How's it going, Frank?" I always knew the answer and that's why I asked the question. He would invariably say, "Every day is a good day. It's just that some days are better."

Isn't that marvelous? And as he said it his face was wreathed in a smile. I'm sure the Lord gave him a grand entry into the Kingdom and now he can indeed say that every day gets better.

What's your attitude on life really like? Take some quiet moments just to look it over, evaluate it and see what it really is. There is always room for a bit more positivism in all our lives. As we enrich it with a better attitude, all those around us will profit from it in grand style.

Let's all polish up our attitudes with some more positivism, joy and cheerfulness; there are lots of people who will be extremely grateful. ✝

All good things come from God

Tuesday was one of those beautiful days that no one could really find any fault with. The temperature was excellent, the sun was shining and everything just seemed to be perfect. I was out on Communion calls and as I was leaving a home an elderly man came walking along. I looked up and said, "You know today certainly is a magnificent day."

He responded cheerfully, "It sure is," and then he added, "I guess God has moved in."

What a tremendous and marvelous response: *God has moved in!*

By that beautiful response, he was saying with deep faith, "All good things come from God and are the outpouring of His generous hand." Or, perhaps he was saying, "Where God is, there is everything that is wonderful."

He surely was right on target, for that is what Heaven is all about, living and dwelling with God, and enjoying the wonders that He manifests so continually.

I don't know who the man was but he surely had things put together and knew where it was all at. He had a marvelous perception of life and a grand approach to a beautiful day.

Attitude is such an important factor in life. We can change the atmosphere of each day by our outlook and approach to the day's activities. When we approach each day with a positive attitude, it becomes bright and sunny, even though it might be a cloudy day. Positivism makes things look much better and brighter, the colors are pinks and bright yellows, and there is an excitement of life.

When the attitude is negative, what a reversal of form there is, and how it affects not only the person, but everyone they encounter. The colors are then dark blues and somber blacks, and certainly there isn't much gaiety, joyousness and exhilaration of life.

We all have within our power to bring a positive joyful approach to daily life. It costs us nothing and the rewards are rich and super abundant. It touches not only our own life but the lives of all of those that we encounter.

I shall never forget this good man I met with that beautiful and charming remark: *I guess God has moved in.* ✝

The fullest dimension of life
will be enjoyed in the halls of eternity

It's a little country cemetery built on the south slope of the hill, only a block distant from the country church. Nearly everyone from the small country parish was buried there, along with all of their relatives, neighbors and friends. It is a holy spot, filled with many memories. I have visited there many, many times over the years because it is the place where my favorite people of this earth are buried, Mother and Dad.

They are buried halfway up the hill, and as I walk the gentle incline of the hill, my mind is filled with a host of memories, the days we shared together starting seventy-two years ago. Memory is that beautiful human facility to recall the wonderful events of the past, to relive them, to re-enjoy them, to experience them once again. My childhood and years of youth were overflowing with much happiness, joy and togetherness in family life. So, it is always with great delight that I recall those bygone events.

Humans not only have the wonderful faculty of remembering but also the beautiful gift of looking forward. As I stand at my parents' graves, many times I recall not only the memories of the past but the anticipation of the glorious things that are to come. The coming Feast of Easter brings to those anticipations a marvelous, glorious, brilliant reality, not only Christ's resurrection but of our own. Every visit to Mother and Dad's grave brings to my soul the wonderful reality that we shall see each other again—not only in the soul, but also in the body, a body that will be filled with the glory, beauty, and charm that only God can give. The soul will give to that body an unbelievable radiance and as Scripture says: *Some will shine like the sun, others like the moon and others like the stars.* (Daniel 12:3)

Easter assures me that the fullest dimension of life, the greatest reality of human experience is not here on Earth, but will be enjoyed in the halls of eternity after we have closed our eyes in death and moved on to meet our God.

The joy of Easter is not reserved for one day but its joys extend throughout all of the days of the year. Its joys give a new dimension to suffering, pain, hardship, trial and tribulation. It gives us assurance that there is meaning to the darkest hours of life and human experience. Though our bodies may be crushed with burdens, our soul can always be lifted up and reassured of the glories and the wonders of our own Easter at the end of time.

Easter is that eternal sun that shines through the darkest clouds of life and illuminates our spirit and soul with the brightness and the glory of the Lord's own resurrection.

My prayer is that the joy of this year's Easter will be shared by you in rich abundance, and that you will carry its joy and assurance into the days, months and years of your continuing life on earth—for Easter is not a day, but is forever. ✝

The Lord said: My grace is enough for you

Everyone loves a winner, and now that the Vikings are 4-and-1, everyone is certainly in their camp and pushing and supporting them. While the Twins ended the 1996 season below .500, their support is not as great or enthusiastic. We have the competitive spirit within us and whether we are playing checkers or bridge, whether it is baseball, football, or trying out for the lead role in a play, we like to be victorious. We like to come out on top.

If we win, somebody else has to lose. There can only be one in first place. You can only have one World Series Champion, one Super Bowl Champion, and one who comes out on top in the presidential race.

There is, however, a race in which everyone can win, everyone can be Number One, and everyone can be a complete victor. That is, of course, the race for Heaven. The race for Heaven is one that everyone can win and anyone can lose. The victors and the losers are determined by each individual person. Each is given adequate tools to work with and sufficient grace and power from God to come out on top. The Lord said to St. Paul: *My Grace is enough for you.* (2 Corinthians 12:9)

Gaining Heaven is the only contest in life that really matters, the only one that is truly significant for the outcome lasts forever. There is no second chance, no rematch. It's a game that we need to play each day with all our hearts, for we never know when it is going to end in death. It could be today, it could be tomorrow, it could be fifty years down the road.

All of this does not need to scare us, but it certainly should make us very sensitive to what is important in life. I often say to myself when the Vikings or the Twins lose, "In the light of Eternity, how important really is this?" To lose a card game, a checkers game or any contest, has only a short term consequence and before many a nightfall, it will have been forgotten.

How are you doing spiritually? Are you playing the spiritual game of life to really win it? Do you make God priority in your lives? Are your religious practices Number One on the drawing board of daily activities?

The things of the world are very passing, very fleeting, and very transitory. Eventually they will crumble to dust and be blown about by the gust of a strong wind.

The Vikings may win the Super Bowl this year, and if they do, all their fans in Minnesota will be extremely happy, including yours truly. But win or lose, it is very small in comparison to my winning the battle of life, to gaining the Crown that lasts forever, to being told by the Lord at the moment of death: *Well done! You are an industrious and reliable servant. Since you were dependable in a small matter I will put you in charge of larger affairs. Come; share your master's joy!* (Matthew 25:21)

That is the supreme reward, above them all. †

We won't pass life's final exam by cramming the night before

June is graduation month, and millions of students reach the various plateaus of their educational experience. Our students graduate from Epiphany in the eighth grade, and then they move onto senior high. Four years later, there will be another graduation ceremony. Some will go to college, and in four years they will gain their degree. Some will proceed to gaining a master's degree or a Ph.D. Each step marks achievement and success in the educational ladder.

After the completion of the various schools and the graduation ceremonies, the individual enters the business or professional world, where again they start at the bottom and begin to rise through their varying accomplishments. The next goal is retirement, a relaxing casual life of doing the varying things they have always wanted to do, but never seemed to have had the time for. Sitting around and not doing much is not very fulfilling or satisfying for many, and so they search for new opportunities and challenges to occupy their time. There is ever a restlessness in the human heart, and rightly so, for the soul of the human person is never fulfilled with all of the material things of the world, its satisfactions and pleasures, but is fulfilled only by that which can fulfill the spirit completely, God Himself.

The greatest graduation ceremony is, of course, the graduation ceremony that transpires at the moment of death, when we leave this earth of ours and move on to that for which we were created, that which is the real purpose of our lives, the Kingdom of Heaven with God. It is the final and the greatest of all graduation exercises, and one that leaves the participant in an eternally fixed state, one of absolute perfect joy, peace and happiness, or one of absolute despair and loss forever. There is no retaking the grand final test of life, for death is entered into but once.

Students work so very, very hard to accomplish their grades, to be able to move on to graduation time, to look back at a job well done and to move forward to new goals and challenges. How hard we all need to work for that grand-daddy of all graduations, the one to Eternal Life. There needs to be daily effort, daily enthusiasm, and daily response to God's call.

No matter what level of the educational process we are in, you can't afford to sit back and do nothing for eight years or four years and then the last few minutes before graduation, expect to put it all back together in instant fashion. You can't microwave education nor should we try to microwave the salvation of our soul.

My prayer is that this graduation time of the year may be a great reminder to each and every one of us to check on how we are doing in our religious school of life. Take some time to examine your status quo. ✝

A retreat is an opportunity
to reaffirm why God placed us here

Quietness massages the soul like the good masseuse massages the tense muscles of the body. Silence is the absence of any sound or noise where as quietness is a tranquility enveloping your whole being. The anxieties of a troubled world are laid aside and one rests in the arms of the Great Creator that fashioned us from nothing.

In this state of quietness there comes to the soul a vision that transcends the elements of time and space and lifts one to the very portals of God's Kingdom, to enjoy a foretaste of our whole purpose of existence. It is an evening on retreat and I am enjoying a slow peaceful walk among the beauties of nature which speak of God's presence everywhere. Magnificent and stately Colorado blue spruce line the road on both sides. They are so perfectly formed with the tops rising with elegance to the great God above. There are robins skipping in the grass to my right, looking for a worm or two, while many other birds are chirping their song of praise to the God above. There is not even a breeze in the air and so the leaves are resting still as death. There are no sounds of violence or turmoil that so harass many city streets, no sounds of quarreling or fighting, all is peaceful, save for a few mosquitoes searching for human blood.

A retreat is a magnificent experience and a time to put aside all of the things of the world and to search for the God who is so ever present; it is just that we are unmindful of Him. A retreat provides a magnificent time to discover anew what life is all about, and how transitory are all of the things of the world. How often, we allow the temporal to overpower us, to be the principal thought that flows within our mind.

A retreat is an opportunity to reaffirm why God placed us on this planet Earth, what direction He wishes us to follow and what interests we are principally to pursue.

The silence of a retreat gives one the opportunity to re-align one's priorities and the essentials of life. It brings to the forefront those things we will want to have cherished, when we are ready to take our last breath and move on to the Kingdom beyond.

Everyone doesn't have the opportunity to take a retreat, but if you do, snatch the opportunity with great enthusiasm. It will be an experience you will never forget or regret. If you are not able to go away on a retreat there are opportunities in which we can gain a good measure of the same benefits. Stay up an hour later some night, alone, or with your spouse, read a selection or two of Scripture, light a candle to remind you of God's presence and then spend some time in quiet personal prayer.

Or on a Saturday or a Sunday evening, begin early and have the entire family involved, shut off all the sound makers in your household, perhaps even take the phone off the hook. Dedicate the time to prayer, perhaps a few hymns that are easy, some Scripture reading or good spiritual book, some favorite prayers and even a short discussion about what the Scripture or other spiritual reading means, and then some quiet time. It will become a refreshing time for the entire family, and will make God's presence more keenly felt, and you will be more fully aware of the unseen guest, Jesus Christ, in your household. You will discover a new spirit, a new respect and reverence of the members of the family for one another. Patience, charity, kindness and unselfishness will gently flow from these gatherings, for where Christ is present there also are His qualities of life.

Give the above a try. You will never regret having done it, and you will be eager to return again and again to the same wonderful experience. St. Augustine said so beautifully, "Our hearts are restless until they rest in God." This is true not only in the Kingdom of Heaven but also here in His Kingdom on Earth. ✝

Discover God wherever you go

We stood on the shores of the Mediterranean Sea, watching the breakers come in with crashing sounds. The white foam was released on the soft sand beach. There were heavy clouds hanging rather precariously overhead and some streaks of lightning illuminated the horizon from east to west.

As one observed a wonder of nature, the power of the sea, you couldn't help but marvel at the power of the Almighty God who holds the universe in the palm of His hand.

For me, the ocean or sea is always the source of much food for thought. We are so small in comparison and so need to continually check our flights into the worlds of pride and vanity. We build so many little sand castles on the sandy shores of life and how quickly they can be washed away in the breakers of sickness, trials and death.

As I watched the on-rushing breakers with their characteristic sounds, my thoughts raced back to our visit to Bethlehem, to the place where the Messiah Jesus was born. It is a place of deep emotion and great sentiment. The spot of His birth is marked by a silver star in the floor. The shepherd's cove, the angels with their chorus of praise, the manger, all were centered on a small baby of six or seven pounds, who was God Himself. The mystery of the Incarnation, God becoming man, the Infinite confined within the limits of the finite, the Almighty limited by the body of a little baby, all of this for my salvation.

A pilgrimage to the Holy Land is an overpowering experience; it provides much opportunity for reflection and mediation. The historical places where Christ walked provide the setting where God walks in the flesh with His human creatures. It is there we experience contrast at its greatest dimension, the infinite and finite touch. Many walk the grounds consecrated by Christ's footsteps but they are not touched, for they have a veil before their eyes.

They are unaware that Christ is the Son of God.

Our faith needs to be continually rekindled, renewed and the Holy Land is a place where that can happen, but it also happens very close to home in our Epiphany Chapel, where there is more than the footprints of Christ but the one who left the footprints, the Lord Himself.

Religion is a relationship with Christ, and the more it deepens, the more perfect will be our direction and perspective in life.

Discover God wherever you go, whether it be the stars on a clear night, the claps of thunder in a summer storm, the magnificent colors of autumn, or the exquisite flakes of a winter snowfall. It isn't only in the breakers of the Mediterranean Sea that we find God. ✝

Pray as if everything depends on God

"Who's in charge?" We often need to ask ourselves that question, "Who's in charge of the great world in which we live?" All we need to do is sit back and listen and watch when a snowstorm comes, or when tornadoes are touching down, or hurricanes are cutting a wide swath along the shoreline of our coast, or when many inches of rain fall in a short time.

All the Lord needs to do is drop a foot or two of snow on the landscape and put some winds in high gear and people quickly realize that they and all of their machines and equipment can be put in a quite helpless position.

We humans like to think we're in charge and we feel that we have many powers and forces that we can control, but when nature unleashes its power, we all need to rather humbly sit back and just watch, listen and admire the forces that God can control with the mere movement of His mind.

I've always loved snowstorms. In our growing up years, it meant a few days off from school, because we didn't have the big trucks and the high powered equipment to quickly clear the roads. We had the horse drawn snowplows that might show up three or four days after the storm was silenced. So winter gave us a few more free days than the students now are able to enjoy. In our mechanized age, a snowstorm really needs to be a dandy to keep people shut in their homes and doing just the wonderful family things that everyone should be doing a lot more of — playing family games, making popcorn, and doing lots of other fun things that families should regularly enjoy.

Getting back to this question I raised earlier about who's in charge? It would be great if we put Jesus Christ in charge of our lives and realized that we shouldn't strive to handle everything by ourselves. We need to accept Christ as our personal Savior and then allow Him take charge of our lives. We need to discontinue a lot of the worries, apprehensions and concerns that so often trouble us and let Christ direct, govern and guide us through the daily channels of human experience. When we let Jesus take charge of our lives we establish some better priorities and principles to guide and govern our varying activities. We should live as He would live if He were in our circumstance or situation. A good principle is to pray as if everything depended on God and work as if everything depended on us.

When we let the Lord control our lives, it's really so much easier and life becomes a "piece of cake." God is awfully good in helping us make the right decisions, doing the appropriate thing in the various activities of life, of choosing the proper ethical solutions to problems or difficulties, to speak and act in the appropriate manner at the appropriate time.

Find a few quiet moments in a quiet spot to sit back, throw off your shoes, close your eyes, and talk to the Lord about how things are going and mention that you would like Him to take charge, to govern and direct your life. Welcome Him into your heart and allow Him to speak in those moments of silence. God speaks the loudest and clearest when our voice is the quietest.

Yes, snowstorms are beautiful realities, and a small one generated some of the thoughts of this Rambling. The Rectory is quiet and outside my window it is quiet except for just a gentle bit of wind. The landscape is clean and white, and the varying lights along the roadways are like beautiful sentinels watching over the pure white landscape. The calm after the storm is a splendid time for reflection. Try it whenever you can. †

Small annoyances can rub like sandpaper

I walked from the church to the rectory and picked up a small little stone in my shoe; immediately there was an irritation to my foot. I endured it until I got to my room but then quickly took off my shoe to remove the little pebble. It was a tiny little thing but it surely made its presence felt.

How true this is in all the various avenues of life. It is not the big things that cause most problems, for they are only here and there in our lives and then we deal with them; but it is the smaller annoyances that are the sandpaper of daily existence.

Mountains are made of little grains of sand and particles of rock and so our lives are constantly fashioned by the little things and so also we affect others by the little things that we say and do.

When we meet the little annoyances of life, we need accept them with patience and with a good spirit in our heart. Compare them to one of the great scenes in the sufferings of Our Lord, this makes them more easily accepted. What is a pebble in my shoe in comparison to having nails driven through my hands and feet or being scourged thirty-nine times with four leather straps? This puts the small annoyance in proper perspective.

So also with our little acts of kindness; what a joy they are to others, and how beautifully they can create a positive and joyous hour in the life of another.

A card I received recently had the following verse:

It's the little things in life
That are God's gifts from above,
It's the little things in life
That fill our hearts with love!

At this writing it is July 31, the Feast of St. Ignatius of Loyola. He was the founder of the Society of Jesus — the Jesuits. He had a great theme for his followers: *All for the greater glory of God.*

What a great motto for our lives as well. Our patient acceptance of annoyance and our sprinkling of each day with kindness will indeed give glory to our Great Father in Heaven.

Why not begin right now! ✝

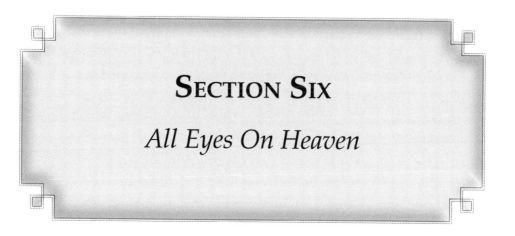

SECTION SIX

All Eyes On Heaven

ALL EYES ON HEAVEN

The Olympic Games come around every two years to capture our attention. The original Olympic Games began in Olympia, Greece, 776 years before Christ was born.

St. Paul, who spent much of his time preaching in historic, athletic and cultural Greece, had the following to say: *Do you not know that the runners in the stadium all run in the race, but only one wins the prize? Run so as to win. Every athlete exercises discipline in every way. They do it to win a perishable crown, but we, an imperishable one.* (1 Corinthians 9:24-25)

The great Apostle surely had his priorities in order.

Olympic hopefuls understand the tremendous amount of time and energy that is involved in order to participate in the Olympics. Most will see their medals slip away quickly, in a matter of just a few seconds. One mistake, one wrong move, and another takes home the glory. But how quickly that glory fades, and names which are household conversation during the Games will not be remembered as the moon changes.

I have often thought what saints we would all be if we expended the energy on the matter of religion and our relationship with God that athletes do in their varying areas of competition.

God gives out all kinds of gold medals and everyone can win one. The award God bestows gives us entry into a joy that never ends — a place called Heaven.

The requirements aren't that tough, either. We simply need a loving heart that shares Christ's love with those we encounter during the expanses of the day, a heart that has allowed Christ to be the Lord of our life.

There can be a gold medal waiting for you at the end of your race, if you wish to attain it. The following Ramblings may help in your training. †

Father Bernard Reiser

Quiet time will do you good

Can you think of a five letter word that starts with "Q" and expresses one of the most necessary aspects or times of human life?

Did you guess it already, or are you peeking ahead to discover the answer? Give up?

The word is QUIET. Even the most casual observer would need to admit that "quiet" is not a very appropriate term to express the typical time that we fast-moving Americans indulge in.

Most homes have a television that has little time to cool off, a radio that can just about rock...rock...rock around the clock, and a hi-fi that is really high on sound.

How often one sees ear phones hooked into some cassette or radio being used by joggers, hikers, or others strolling down the avenue. We live in a world so filled with sound and noise that quiet seems such a precious and necessary ingredient of life.

I sometimes think we are afraid of quiet and the searching that results from quiet, a time to reflect on the priorities and principles of life, a time to think about God, eternity, the destiny of life after this life, an opportunity of just asking oneself: "Where am I really going and what's this whole thing called 'life' all about?"

A. P. Gouthey has a great deal of wisdom packed into the following quotation. Give it the courtesy of some serious reflection:

"Character is not built by battling and excitement alone. The harvest is not ripened by the thunderous forces of nature, but by the secret silent invisible forces. So the best qualities of our spiritual lives are matured by quietness, silence and commonplace."

Do yourself a favor; find some quiet time each day. ✝

Make your faith about helping others

As of this writing, the Twins are in last place in the American League West, but still only a game and a half out of first place.

My, oh my, the negative comments I have heard this past week about the Twins. All the prophets of doom are busy hanging lots of black crepe. When the Twins were winning the World Series, they were the greatest ever and the words of praise rolled like a mighty river across the State of Minnesota. We were NUMBER ONE! Top of the heap! World Champions! Everyone got into the act to share the glory.

I guess it's a lot like that with life in general. The winners take all, and the losers are just plain losers. The successful, the charming, the talented, the gifted, ride the high waves of glory, praise and fanfare. Those not quite so pretty, those who learn rather slowly, those who have never known the spotlight or anywhere near first place, suffer in silence and in the shadows of oblivion. What heavy crosses they often carry and how lonely their lives become as they trudge the paths of daily endurance.

We need to be sensitive to those people and extend to them some special attention. They live in all our neighborhoods; they come to our church and often walk out alone to their cars. They attend our social functions and various meetings and activities. They will usually sit alone or on the fringes. They may not be great conversationalists or have the most vibrant personalities, but they have hearts filled with love and loneliness.

God loves them as He loves each person with an infinite love.

The above people are waiting for you to make the first move, to take the first step, to say the first word in building a friendship with them.

Are you willing to make that first move, to make your Christianity more than a set of beliefs but also a way of acting?

Break out of your clique! Many grand people are waiting for you. †

Can we come up with a 'clutch play' in the game of life?

The Minneapolis *Star Tribune* had the following quote in a sports article written by Dennis Brackin on July 15, 1994: "The Twins were 2-for-18 with runners in scoring position, giving them a three-game total of 4-for-38 (.105) with runners in scoring position.

"The Twins have lost all three of those games, as well as 18 of their last 24.

"Two-for-18, that says it all."

Twins center fielder Kirby Puckett said, "What more can I say? Two-for-18, that's pretty explanatory."

"The Twins' perspective of the American League Central Division race had changed dramatically as a result of their repeated failure in clutch situations. Minnesota is 17-for-97 (.175) with runners in scoring position in 11 games this month, nine of them losses."

Being a Twins fan, Brackin's words were certainly less than comforting, yet unmistakingly true. When I laid down the paper, I thought to myself, "How often we are in those clutch situations in the various experiences of life?" We frequently have the opportunity of really scoring big in our ascent to God by following the Christian way of life, but how often we blow the opportunities by striking out by our lack of patience, charity or kindness.

During the course of every day we often have a spiritual runner on third base and our patience is being tested rather severely and we lose a beautiful opportunity of scoring some great spiritual points for Heaven by yelling, screaming and blowing our top instead of turning our mind to the crucifixion scene of the Lord on Calvary and seeing how His patience under unbelievable stress is a living example for us in many circumstances.

There are many occasions when we could have a wonderful spiritual hit by being kind and charitable in our speech when others are being unkind. There are opportunities to say the good word, the thoughtful word, but we chose to say something negative, unkind, or uncharitable.

Then there are those times when we know that we have had enough to drink and one or two more are going to push us over the edge and make us dangerous to ourselves as well as to others and we ground out, thinking within ourselves, "Well, just this one time, I'll have one more."

We can all name dozens of different circumstances when we struck out, flied out, grounded out in those spiritual opportunities where we could have made a solid hit or even a home run by doing the right thing by following the right code of ethics, doing what Jesus would want us to do in that particular circumstance.

The road to sainthood isn't usually just one great heroic act of the will like martyrdom. Normally it is made up of those countless little things we can do day after day to make a hit for God. Keep your eyes open for those little spiritual moments when we can step forth for God, manifest our faith and do the right thing. Our hit will encourage others to do the same. Our success influences others to make good choices.

We can find inspiration just about anywhere, even in reading the sports page on a Friday morning. St. Paul once said: *So whether you eat or drink or whatever you do, do everything for the glory of God.* (1 Corinthians 10:31)

He might have added, "Even reading the sports page," had there been one in his day. Who knows? †

Those we love need to be the first recipients of our kindness

The last one in line. What am I talking about, the last one in line? Well, very pointedly, I'm referring to those who usually are the last ones to be the recipients of our kindness, our thoughtfulness, our goodness, our compliments, the special little things that we offer to people during our walk in life.

How often we are so generous with our compliments to people we work with, associate with, people perhaps in the neighborhood, or in this or that social gathering. We notice the special things they do, or the special things about them and are quick to give a word of praise. On the other hand, how slow we oftentimes are in complimenting and praising those who are the closest to us, our loved ones, members of our family, and members of our immediate household. How frequently they are the ones who we take for granted, the ones we feel will always be there and don't need the extra special little words of kindness and commendation.

As a clergyman, I have had the opportunity to attend many visitations and funerals, and there are always so many magnificent flowers around and no one could love flowers any more than I do. Each time I see those wonderful colorful blossoms, I say to myself, "I wonder how many flowers this person ever received during their lifetime?"

There is an old saying: *A rose bud in life is worth ten dozen after you're gone.* It brings us back to the basic truth that it is much better to give to people while they're still alive, whether it's a single flower, a small gift, a piece or two of candy, or a sincere compliment. It's those little things of life that really make the difference, and they make the sun shine even though it's cloudy. They bring radiant beams of light where otherwise there might be darkness.

Those we love need to be the first recipients of our kindness, our goodness, our compliments, our gifts, our little expressions of love, devotion, tenderness and attention. Don't wait until tomorrow. Why not start today? Lay this Rambling down right now, go and do something nice or say something generous, kind or thoughtful to that person who is special in your life, that person whom you love. Make a big difference to them and it will give you a great feeling in your heart.

Those special people in our homes need to be first in line, not last. †

Warmth eventually melts the coldest ice

His name is Claw and he's a tom cat weighing twenty pounds. As far as cats go, he's a very attractive animal. His black fur along with various other shades of color and some beautiful white patches, give him a very distinctive and attractive appearance. Claw takes up residence at a home where I go to offer Communion every Tuesday morning. He definitely is not the friendliest of creatures I have ever encountered and every time I come to the house, he will be sitting on one of the chairs or the sofa peering with sinister eyes upon me as I approach the living room. He obviously doesn't want much to do with me and his appearance warranted that particular impression.

The home care nurses who care for the wife have on their charts, "beware of cat." Not a bad bit of advice because I had been warned not to touch or pet Claw or I may find myself with a bloody hand or more cat than I would like to cope with on a Tuesday morning.

Claw holds his distance every week and I make no unnecessary or foolish approaches to him. As long as he keeps to his side of the room and me to mine, we remain relatively good friends.

Weeks moved into months and months into years and thus it went this way between Claw and me for two long years — Claw dominating his end of the room and I mine. But I always manage a smile and a kindly expression for him, trying to let him know that I hold no antagonism and wouldn't mind being sociable friends. I figured that if St. Francis of Assisi could be great friends of all of the various animals of the field, I might try to walk the same path as the great man from Assisi. They say that animals can sense when you are afraid and I must admit I had really no fear of Claw.

Then, miracle of miracles happened about a month ago. Dear Claw strolled over alongside of me as I was giving Communion to the couple. He rolled over on his back and looked up with the most inviting eyes in the world, as if to say, "Why don't you pet me or scratch my stomach?" He went into those playful maneuvers of asking me to be friends, which I of course did at a moment's notice. He showed great acceptance and joy in my response and since then we have been great friends and have had a marvelous relationship, one with the other.

There are oftentimes humans — similar to Claw the cat — who seem so unapproachable and distant; they appear to have their own agenda or attitude of, "Don't try to get to me." We never know what circumstances bring people to that point of human behavior but we can't just write them off and have nothing to do with them. We need to try to break through that outside shell and discover that they are really special people, individuals with lots of wonderful qualities and much goodness hiding behind a past hurt or misunderstanding. We need to be patient with them, kind, thoughtful, waiting for that appropriate moment when they will lay aside their defenses and their brick walls and open their hearts in loving and thoughtful kindness.

Continued warmth will eventually melt the coldest ice, and so also kindness, thoughtfulness and goodness will break down the coldness of any individual.

Claw and I are good friends now and I look forward to seeing him every Tuesday morning. He rolls over on his back, looks at me with those big wonderful cat eyes, and is just waiting to play a bit and show me that he rather likes who I am.

Thanks, Claw, for inspiring my Rambling for the week. If it hadn't been for you, there may have been an empty column here, and that would have really been bad news. †

Kindness melts the ice
of anger and animosity

Spring is a wonderful, glorious time of the year and after a long cold winter, how refreshing it is to go out and bask in the beautiful rays of a spring sun. The snow banks gradually melt under the power of the sun. The thickest ice, step by step, gives way to the unrelenting warmth from above. Rivulets of water run here and there, forming ever widening streams, until they finally join the rush of the rivers.

The frozen earth slowly thaws, and soon the dandelions begin to green, and how we enjoyed those dandelion greens in early spring; they made a magnificent salad. The crocus and the tulip begin to push their little green shoots through the earth to capture the warmth and the light of the sun. Soon they will unfold in the first blossoms of spring to the delight of those who are tired of slipping and sliding over the ice and snow of winter. Trees and bushes begin to form their gentle little buds that will break forth into the wonderful leaves of spring. Lawns become a marvelous carpet of green, and wherever you look, there is the freshness and exhilaration of new life.

What a wonderful reality is the sun in our universe. Without it, we would be locked into cold, snow and frozen earth and we would live in a world of darkness. What the sun is to our earth, kindness is to the world of people. Kindness is love in action, love expressed, love being vibrantly lived in the lives of humans. Kindness melts the ice of anger and animosity. Kindness wipes away the snow of unkindness. It thaws the frozen earth of sullenness, despair and despondency. Under its influence, flowers of happiness, joy, peace and contentment blossom in grand array.

Kindness melts the coldest heart and the most stubborn will. It nurtures the best in people. It breaks down the walls of separation and the hedges of indifference. Kindness makes life more worthwhile, and opens the lines of communication and togetherness among people.

As you bask in the beautiful sunshine of the springtime that is beginning to surround us, may it remind us of another sunshine that you and I can bring into our daily lives, the sunshine of kindness. It will work wonders beyond our imagination. It will create a new world of excitement around you, and you will be a welcomed guest at every gathering, for you will emanate goodness, cheerfulness, joyousness.

There is no charge for kindness. It is something that each and every one of us can share with those we meet. It flows from a loving heart and is a beautiful response to our Lord's admonition, "to love one another as He loves us."

Kindness makes Christ visible in our present age and it allows our fellow humans to see that Christianity is more than worship in church; it is also a way of life, the way you and I treat each other.

I pray that the sun of kindness may always be very bright and warm in the heart of each of us. ✝

It takes a strong person
to do what is right

What do you think is the greatest pressure in all the world? You hear people talking about PSIs (pounds per square inch), or the pressure that is exploded in a hydrogen bomb that wipes out everything in its path. People speak about being under pressure, which causes nervousness, tensions, grey hair and upset stomachs.

What I think is one of the greatest pressures in all the world is peer pressure. It is the force that is exerted upon us to do things a certain way or to speak a certain way by the influence of the people around us. We have our peers at work, in our community, in our social activities, at school and even within our family relationships. We all have tremendous peer pressure in the various areas and activities of our lives, and when those pressures are to do something wrong (when we know we should do something good) it is very, very difficult to go against the stream. We often hear people talk about the peer pressure teens are under, but really everybody has peer pressure — mothers, dads, business people, workers; those gathering in their little social groups are all under peer pressure.

Women have peer pressure when gathering in their groups or circles and when everyone else starts gossiping, it is extremely difficult not to share and join in the destructive words. Men have a difficult time bucking the stream of those telling dirty stories or those encouraging others to have one more drink before going home. Business people have difficulty going against some practices that others are engaged in that aren't very honest or just. Teens continually struggle against the pressures of using drugs, alcohol or the misuse of sexuality — *everyone else is doing it so why shouldn't I?*

John the Baptist stood alone against Herod for living with his brother's wife while all the rest of the nation remained silent. Herod ordered the beheading of John the Baptist because he couldn't take the pressure of the power people who were with him at the dinner.

It takes a strong person to stand against the wave of peer pressure and do what is right, or speak what is correct, while being alone in a field of opposition. It is at those times we test the strength of our faith and the fortitude that is within our soul. We need God's Grace to do the right thing, and we gain that power and strength of Grace in the Mass, the Sacraments and in our quiet private prayer.

When we stand for what is right and just, others will gain strength from our position, and they too will have a greater ease in following the right path.

Don't let peer pressure overpower you, for with God's grace and a strong will, we can stem the tide of peer pressure to do wrong, and instead do right and be like sentinels of virtue in a world that needs goodness so desperately. ✝

Four ingredients make for a happy home

I never wrote a recipe for a cookbook in my life but I surely enjoy eating the results of those wonderful recipes. An excellent dinner and a good dessert go a long way toward making us all more content. It must be okay with the Lord because He gave such a marvelous flavor to so many foods and gave us a sense of taste to enjoy them in a delightful manner.

Our housekeeper Rae does an excellent job in the kitchen and certainly makes mealtime a very enjoyable and magnificent occasion. Bakers Square is really challenged by her pies, cakes, cookies and bread.

I do have a recipe, however; it's a recipe for a happy home. I call it A HAPPY HOME. There are four wonderful ingredients to this happy home recipe and if you and your family were to try them for a few weeks, you would quickly discover that they have the power to change the atmosphere within your household in a very positive fashion. The four ingredients are: P, K, NY and O.

The P stands for family prayer and by that I don't mean just the quick, before-mealtime blessing but three to five minutes daily, with everyone gathering together and putting God in the center and sharing a little time with the God who is ever present. Closing with the Lord's Prayer and each holding hands with the other brings togetherness and a unity that only the Lord can build. It's pretty difficult to fight and battle when you're joining hands and hearts in prayer.

The K stands for kindness. What a wonderful element kindness is in daily life. We could literally change the world, each and every one of us, if we were committed to one act of kindness within our household each day. The Christophers have the old motto, "Light a candle to scatter the darkness." A kindness within our home by each member will do much to bring joy, peace and harmony.

The NY stands for no yelling. No raising of voices, no shouting, no screaming, just use that calm tempered voice that is like the sound of the cool breeze in summer that refreshes and heals. Saint James tells us: *He who sins not with the tongue is the perfect person.* (James 1:26) As we look into our own lives, how frequently we discover a raised voice causes much disturbance.

The O stands for obedience. Every son and daughter should show a respectful and reverent obedience to their parents. The child Jesus, who was son of God, went back to Nazareth and was subject to Mary and Joseph. If the Lord God Himself could be subject to those two humans, how we need to be subject to those who have given us life and cared for us during those many years when we were so utterly dependent on their love and generosity.

I would challenge each family to use this simple little recipe for a happy home. I know that you will discover it to be a way and a means of bringing more joy, peace, happiness, and togetherness to that wonderful little family circle that is yours. The family is the basic cell of society. When those in our families are happy and prayerful, loving and giving, it soon spills over into all of society.

To each and every one of you I wish a happy home. God bless you all. †

Give marriage the attention it deserves

There are certain virtues that I believe are essential for a peaceful, happy marriage, resulting in many wonderful years together.

The first of those virtues is *Kindness*.

Kindness is a wonderful and beautiful quality in which we reach out to others in a multiplicity of ways. The kind word, the kind deed, the kind thought — all of these give our spouse a sense of worth, dignity and well-being. As one looks at the life of Jesus, He was the personification of kindness. He was always reaching out in different ways to those around Him. He touched the hearts of children and the elderly; those carrying heavy burdens and those filled with the joys of life. He was in every respect a kindly person. And so in the marriage relationship, there needs to be a continual expression of kindness between spouses, something that needs to happen many times a day. Try for at least three acts of kindness every day; those acts of kindness will set a beautiful stage for a happier and more contented marriage.

The second of those virtues is *Patience*.

We need to be patient and discipline ourselves. If we don't discipline ourselves, how can we ever hope to help others in the manner of advice or suggestion? The storming sea stirs up the ocean, but the tranquil sea offers a smooth surface in which all seems well. There should never be yelling, screaming or shouting in a marriage relationship. We need to control our voices, be moderate in our speech and controlled in everything we say and do. One can control their temper if they set their mind to it. The Book of Proverbs has a beautiful saying: *A patient man is better than a warrior, and he who rules his temper, better than he who takes a city.* (Proverbs 16:32)

Thirdly there needs to be *Love*.

Love means sacrifice; it means placing the needs of others ahead of one's own needs. Jesus said: *No one has greater love than this, to lay down one's life for one's friends.* (John 15:13) To lay down one's life means to put the needs of your spouse ahead of your own.

Our Lord showed us perfect love on the cross when He gave Himself fully and completely for us. We live in a world of selfishness in which we are encouraged to fufill our own needs, satisfy our own cravings, and all other things come second. What a different world it would be if everyone thought first of other people and placed themselves second! We can start this within our own homes.

I ask couples to celebrate their wedding anniversary each month so that if they married on the twelfth of the month, every month on the twelfth they would celebrate. The man would bring his wife a long-stem rose. There is a beauty and a charm in a single rose and the large red ones are exquisite. What a joy this will bring to every woman as her husband offers her a special rose every month! The wife, on the other hand, should prepare a special meal on that same day. They will sit down together with the flower in the middle of the table to enjoy a wonderful meal that she has prepared to set the tone that their marriage is something very wonderful to celebrate. This is not a great thing, but it is a meaningful and a necessary practice.

We often fail to express the love that rises up within our hearts. Do something each day to make your marriage special. Otherwise, the relationship will fade. The plant that is not watered and nourished soon withers and dies. Love that is not nourished by all of these various qualities, virtues and gifts soon withers. Someday, the couple may find they just don't love each other any longer; their love was destroyed by lack of attention. I recommend reading a passage in the Book of Colossians, 3:12-15. Read it frequently; it will remind you of these beautiful virtues and qualities that God wants you to instill into your daily life.

Finally, couples need to pray together every day. It is only with God's help and grace that we can accomplish anything good and worthwhile on this Earth. Daily prayer together is essential for any couple. God Bless you and have a happy and wonderful life together. It's all in your hands. †

Gaining the Kingdom
is all that really counts

I have always enjoyed reading proverbs, adages, maxims, old sayings, bits of wisdom or whatever you wish to call them. My friend, Tony, gave me a very thoughtful, provoking one last week. Here it is: *Worry is the interest paid in advance for things that may never happen.*

How much interest have you flushed down the drain that could have well been avoided? The past is gone and irreversible, no matter from what angle you approach it. The future is, as it states, future; it will never be lived for we can only live the present moment. The present moment I can handle, for it comes at me only one second at a time, so why should I worry or have any fear.

Our Lord has a multitude of great sayings and admonitions in the Bible but a real gem is: *Do not live in fear, little flock. It has pleased your Father to give you the Kingdom.* (Luke 12:32)

How's that for a great tranquilizer. Gaining the Kingdom is all that really counts and the Heavenly Father has that in store for us, so why sweat the little things.

Worry is like a black cloud that hides the sunshine of happiness, and etches the face with apprehension instead of smiles.

The Lord has more to say: *Consider the ravens: they do not sow, they do not reap, they have neither cellar nor barn—yet God feeds them. How much more important you are than the birds! Which of you by worrying can add a moment to his life span? If the smallest things are beyond your power, why be anxious about the rest? Or take the lilies; they do not spin, they do not weave; but I tell you, Solomon in all his splendor was not arrayed like any one of them. If God clothes in such splendor the grass of the field, which grows today and is thrown on the fire tomorrow, how much more will he provide for you, O weak in faith! It is not for you to be in search of what you are to eat or drink. Stop worrying. The unbelievers of this world are always running after these things. Your Father knows that you need such things. Seek out instead His kingship over you, and the rest will follow in turn.* (Luke 13:24-31)

I always felt I had a little more on the stick than the ravens, and if they get taken care of, I guess, that should put any of my worries to rest.

Have a nice day, and please, *don't pay any interest in advance!* †

There is nothing that cuts like a sharp tongue

When I was in Spain a few years ago, I bought a sword that was patterned after the sword used by El Cid, the famed Spanish warrior. It's a deadly instrument, and if someone were to plunge it through your chest, it would surely bring life's activities to a very abrupt end.

There is another sword that is even more deadly than the sword of steel that can destroy the body and that is the sword of the tongue; it can destroy so much in the character and reputation of many. The tongue is a marvelous instrument, but one that has a tremendous potential for both good and evil. It can be used in so many wonderful ways to express love, devotion, affection and kindness. It can speak words of encouragement to lift up, and to support, and to soothe the downhearted.

On the other hand, it can be one of the most destructive members that we have within our bodies. There is nothing so cutting as a sharp tongue, nothing as destructive as the tongue of one who assassinates and destroys the reputation, the character and feelings of others.

The tongue is also often used in a very disrespectful, dehumanizing fashion, such as when people use words and phrases that pierce the heart and destroy feelings and emotions. Someone said to me last week, and I quote: "I can't believe the disrespect that people show to one another, by the words they use and the manner in which they attack one another." How often this is true, even within family circles, between spouses, or between children and parents. How often degrading and dehumanizing words and expressions are used along with filthy and suggestive terminology that so insult the human person.

St. James tells us: *If anyone offend not in word, the same is a perfect person.* How close he was to the mark on that statement.

We might all very well examine our speech and how we speak to those who sit around our own dinner tables, those who are members of our immediate family. Are they the recipients of loving words and uplifting language, or are they the victims of degrading speech, insulting words, and dehumanizing expressions?

Why not check out how well you can rate yourself in your use of speech? Surely the tongue that receives the body and blood of Jesus Christ should be one that is free of sin and used in a holy and uplifting manner.

They say a word to the wise is sufficient. I hope my words haven't been too numerous to touch your hearts. †

Willingness to say 'no' could help us

It's only a two-letter word, but one that becomes extremely meaningful in the life of the human person. It is one of the first words that children learn in their earlier years of speaking, and they say it with great firmness, determination and much zest. It's also a word that we adults need to use far more frequently and regularly in the course of daily living — a word that frequently can spell either salvation or damnation. Have you guessed the word? I'm sure you have by now. The word is NO.

Children can be very firm in their expression of NO when parents and others want them to do something, eat a particular food, go to bed, or a dozen other little scenes that involve the little jewels. It would be a great asset in our adult spiritual lives if we used the word NO in many more situations that we encounter.

In our spiritual life, the willingness to say NO in many situations would certainly be for our greater benefit. The need to say NO to the devil and all of the forces of evil may occur many times during a single day; how frequently we are invited by our passions, our senses, or the world at large to do what is sinful. Saying NO to these many temptations, or invitations to sin, demands a real sterling character, an abundance of God's grace, and a willingness on our part to follow the right path of life.

It is too easy to say YES to the extra drink that will be one too many or to say YES to drugs when many of our peers are using. It is no small challenge to say NO to sinful sexual relationships when a YES is so pleasurable and easy. How easy it is to gossip while others are doing the same, or to lie when truth is a bit difficult. Saying NO to dishonesty is a challenge when others are being dishonest in the workplace.

The Ten Commandments are basically commands by Almighty God to say NO to many things that are not permitted or are obstacles on the path to eternal glory. God's strong words

Thou Shalt Not are certainly very firm, expressive and to the point.

Lent is a wonderful time of year when we develop a greater ability to say NO. Saying NO at the right time is a matter of spiritual discipline and Lent is time to strengthen that ability to say NO at very strategic times when sin is involved and our salvation may be on the line. Our whole general welfare may be in need of a firm and definite NO.

Growth in our spiritual life can be simply expressed — learn to say NO to sin and YES to Jesus. This makes a wonderful combination that adds up to Heaven forever. ✝

Put God first when filling up your day

True success in life is gained by keeping our priorities straight and giving those priorities a first position in our daily lives. They need be focal points and give direction to our daily life. The following was left in my mail box by someone, and I really don't know who it was. I made a few adaptations of what was given me and here is the result.

I was reading about an expert on the subject of time management. One day this expert was speaking to a group of business students and professionals. To drive home a point, he used an illustration I'm sure those students and professionals will never forget. After I share it with you, I hope you'll never forget it either.

As this man stood in front of the group of high-powered overachievers, he said, "Okay, time for a quiz." Then he pulled out a one-gallon, wide-mouthed Mason jar and set it on a table in front of him. Then he produced about a half dozen rocks that just fit through the jar's mouth and carefully placed them, one at a time, into the jar. When the jar was filled to the top and no more rocks would fit inside, he asked the class "Is this jar full?"

Everyone in the class said, "Yes."

Then he said, "Really?" He reached under the table and pulled out a bucket of gravel. Then he dumped some gravel in and shook the jar causing pieces of gravel to work themselves down into the spaces between the big rocks. Then he smiled and asked the group once more, "Is the jar full?" By this time the class was onto him.

"Probably not," one of them answered.

"Good!" he replied. And he reached under the table and brought out a bucket of sand. He started dumping the sand in and it went into all the spaces left between the rocks and the gravel. Once more he asked the question, "Is this jar full?"

"No!" the class shouted.

Once again he said, "Good!" Then he grabbed a pitcher of

water and began to pour it in until the jar was filled to the brim. Then he looked up at the class and asked, "What is the point of this illustration?"

One eager beaver raised his hand and said, "The point is, no matter how full your schedule is, if you try really hard, you can always fit some more things into it."

"No," the speaker replied, "that's not the point." The truth this illustration teaches us is: if you don't put the big rocks in first, you'll never get them in at all."

What are the "big rocks" in your life? The goals of your life that YOU want to accomplish? To gain the eternal joys of Heaven, to daily walk with God, to be faithful in church attendance and reception of the sacraments, to build a strong family life by time and dedication, to be unselfish, to give and be kind to your loved ones, to be responsible in your job?

Remember to put these BIG ROCKS in first or you'll never get them in at all. So, tonight, or in the morning, when you are reflecting on this short story, ask yourself these questions: What are the "big rocks" in my life? What are my priorities? Are they the correct priorities? Do those priorities fulfill the great purpose of why God made me — to know Him, love Him, serve Him and to be with Him forever in the next life? Those are the Big Rocks; put them first into your jar of life! †

Lent gives us a wonderful opportunity to focus the vision God gave us

There is an interesting reality about Michelangelo, the great Italian sculptor. Before he began to sculpture a work of art, he would prayerfully sit before the piece of marble to be used and reflect on the image he wished to sculpt, such as his magnificent Pietà (Vatican's St. Peter's Basilica), Moses (Italy's Basilica of St. Peter in Chains), or David (Florence, Italy). When he could picture the figure clearly in the marble he would begin to chisel away at the irrelevant material until the image in his mind was transformed in the stone. He fashioned magnificent pieces of art because he saw precisely in his mind what he wished to create.

We all need to be people of vision, individuals who have the great vision given to us by Christ: Attaining the kingdom of Heaven and living with Jesus, in company with the Father and the Holy Spirit. This vision gives us the great purpose of our life on earth and all other attainments are secondary — at the end of life they are meaningless.

It is by deep personal prayer that we fashion the eternal image in our personal lives until it becomes the very focus of our lives. We need to see it as the only real purpose of our lives, and that all other experiences of life are to focus around it. Like Michelangelo chipping away the rock to create the image within his mind, so we need to chip away worldly and materialistic elements that hinder our journey to God and the attainment of Heaven.

The bible says it so well in Chapter One of Ecclesiastes:

Vanity of vanities, says Qoheleth,
Vanity of vanities! All things are vanity!
What profit has man from all the labor
Which he toils at under the sun?
One generation passes and another comes,
But the world forever stays.

With the beginning of Lent, we have a wonderful opportunity to focus on the vision Christ has given us. The fulfillment of the vision leads down a path that is highlighted with penance, self denial, fasting and worship within the community. It is graced with good works, kindness, charity, and unselfishness.

We all have a lot of chipping to do, to make the vision of Heaven clearly expressed in our lives. As we realize more deeply the Pearl of Great Price, we need to make it the primary focus of our life, for it is the one vision of our life that is eternal.

With every blow or tap on his chisel, Michelangelo brought the image within his mind closer to reality in the marble. We with every passing moment of our lives, bring our vision of Heaven closer to reality as well. ✝

God remembers all
our little acts of kindness

Yes, I have nearly finished receiving 365 great big gifts from Almighty God, and that isn't all of it. Each of those gifts were then divided into twenty-four smaller gifts and those twenty-four smaller gifts were in turn divided into sixty smaller gifts and then those sixty gifts were again divided into sixty more gifts and those small little gifts were seconds. The really big gifts were the days and then the days were divided into hours and the hours were divided into minutes and the minutes were divided into seconds and each of those little seconds of life are a precious and un-equaled gift from God Almighty. Without those gifts we could not enjoy any other gift, for without life nothing else can be enjoyed.

We often take this gift of life so much for granted, and as the days slip into months, the months into years and years into de-cades, we then begin looking at ourselves in the mirror and we notice that the lines of age are showing, the hair is turning gray, our feet are not as swift as they were before nor are our fingers as limber as we would like them.

Every moment of life is a golden opportunity of storing up something very special and precious for the next life. Once that moment is gone, the opportunity is gone as well, lost forever. As we look at the seconds of life, and if we are wise and prudent individuals, we will want to lay up, for ourselves treasures that last forever. The bible says: *Store up heavenly treasure, which neither moths nor rust corrode nor thieves break in and steal.* (Matthew 6:20)

As I check the death book for 1995, I noticed that ninety-one people have died this year. Their moments of opportunity have ended. They no longer have that golden chance that you and I have day after day.

God pays wonderful interest rates, rates that far exceed anything we could possibly imagine here on earth. The wonderful thing about the God who rewards and blesses us is that He doesn't miss a trick. The littlest act of kindness, the shortest prayer, the smile, the word of encouragement, the patient suffering of an annoyance or an irritation, pain borne with acceptance, all of those wonderful little things that cross our paths day after day, the Lord sees them all. He doesn't need to write them down, they are indelibly recorded in His infinite memory bank, and then when we come to leave this dear old earth we so cherish, and He will have lots and lots of surprises for us.

He will say, "Do you remember?"

And we'll say, "Really I don't."

He will say, "Do you remember this or that little thing you did for a child, for the elderly, the one who was discouraged and despondent, or the downtrodden? Do you remember the helping hand you gave to someone who really needed you, or the prayer you offered for someone in distress?"

We'll be surprised that He didn't miss a one of them and will bless us with rich abundance.

Our repented sins He will have buried in the depths of the sea and He will remember them no longer, but the good things will be indelibly etched in God's infinite memory bank.

As another year slips away, and a new one soon will begin, I will be a little more attentive to those little moments of time and the wonderful opportunities they present to me day after day. If I capture them and use them rightly, God will remember them and He will have surprises to share with me when I close my eyes, say goodbye to Mother Earth, and open them to the Kingdom of Heaven. †

It takes conviction to be a beacon in a sea of darkness

The voice of the mob is not a criteria for right or wrong, for justice or the lack of justice. It is easy to go along with the voice of the mob, where shoulder to shoulder everyone is echoing the same sympathies, thoughts, principles, or lack of them. Our individuality is often lost in the pressure of the mob and in great numbers of people. It takes very little courage to move along with the sea of humanity, when it affirms or disclaims any particular cause.

These thoughts were prompted as I recalled the great drama of Palm Sunday, when our Lord rode into Jerusalem on the donkey and the townspeople spread their coats and palm branches before Him, and cried out, "Hosanna to the Son of David." Within a week's time those same people would be crying out, "Crucify Him! Crucify Him!"

The feelings, the emotions, the climate had dramatically changed. The high priest, and the others in leadership, fanned the great movement of antagonism against the Lord Jesus, and those who had been singing the Hosannas were now chanting the cry for crucifixion. How quickly the crowd can be moved and swayed from one side of an issue to another, depending upon who is calling the shots.

It takes a person of strong principles and deep convictions to stand against the chanting of the crowd, and alone embrace the cause of justice, righteousness and goodness. It is so very, very easy to be pious when everyone else is pious. It is no challenge to uphold goodness when all those about are adopting the very same thing. It is a quite different matter when you stand as the lone sentinel amidst the crowd; the only beacon in the sea of darkness; the only one with conviction to stand against the sway of a crowd that is promoting a matter that is evil.

All of us have many opportunities, during the course of any particular week, to stand up for Christ, to be that solitary one who follows the dictates of a good conscience, who upholds the laws of God and the teachings of Jesus. The charitable tongue is not too welcome among those who are backbiting, gossiping and slandering. Honesty is a real challenge when injustice abounds, where corners are cut, unfair allowances made, and where the cause of justice is not kept. How easy it is to justify immorality under the pretense that everyone else is doing it.

The Ten Commandments are not suggestions or a summary of what the Jewish people formulated. They are commands set down by God Himself.

Palm Sunday has a powerful message, a strong teaching. It certainly is one we can all carry within our hearts: Stand up for what is God's will, regardless of the numbers who do or don't. ✝

The Lord deserves your very best

When I was a priest in White Bear Lake at St. Mary of the Lake, there was a man named Jacques who came to daily Mass. He was always dressed with great detail and looked as if he was going to a grand ball. I asked him one day, "Jacques, I noticed that you are always dressed so beautifully for daily Mass and I am really inspired by that."

He responded very quickly by saying, "If I were to go and meet the governor today, I would certainly dress in my very best to show my respect for his position in government. When I go to communion, I am receiving the King of Kings and certainly He deserves the very best that I can offer."

There is another dimension to this story; Jacques made his living by operating a horse stable. He was up each morning early, feeding and tending to the horses and the barns, and then he changed clothes to come in for the early Mass. So, his was not a reality of merely stopping by on the way to the office when he came dressed in great style.

I am in no way indicating that those who come to daily Mass so faithfully here at Epiphany need to be dressing up in their Sunday best. It is an inspiration to me that so many come to attend Mass and receive Holy Communion on their way to work. They make a great sacrifice in getting up early and coming over for that special religious treat. The Lord loves work clothes as well as Sunday fashions. It is our heart — not our attire — that matters.

In thinking of Jacques, though, my thoughts were more toward those attending Mass on Saturday evening or Sunday morning. At times, one wonders if perhaps there might be a little more discretion used by some as to the style and type of attire they have on. The Lord certainly isn't looking for elegant or expensive clothes, but I do believe that modesty must always be a prime concern so that our attire is in no way a source of temptation or distraction to others. What is appropriate on the beach or at various forms of entertainment may not be exactly the best choice for Sunday worship. Those who come in work clothes on the way to or from work are most welcome and should not be embarrassed. God knows your circumstance.

We live in an age in which reverence and respect has suffered considerably, and we need to be continually on the alert to protect, respect and reverence that which is holy and sacred. We live in a very casual society, but we need to be cautious that casualness does not slip into the realm of the sacred and the sublime.

Be attentive to what you wear to church and watch the attire of those for whom you are responsible.

I often think of Jacques and his respect and reverence for the person of Jesus in the Eucharist. He was always an inspiration to me. My recollection of him has made me more attentive to the respect and reverence I need to have for the great person of Jesus Christ who comes to me in Holy Communion, and how I need to realize that it is a person I receive and not a wafer of bread. I never really adequately thanked Jacques for the inspiration he was to me, but I am sure that he knows it in the Kingdom, where he sees Jesus face to face. Now he knows perfectly who it was that he received as he walked the aisle to Communion. Thanks, Jacques, and remember me before the Lord. ✝

Speak and act like Christians; people will notice

My mother had lots of good advice to give us children. It was down to earth, practical, and of course, had a Christian orientation. As I was leaving the farm for college, she had a beautiful reminder, very simple and to the point: "Please don't ever embarrass the Reiser name."

Very clearly she reminded me that as I lived, conducted myself, spoke and responded, the reputation of the family was at stake. Would I please realize that the reputation the family had fashioned over the years should not be torn down by some foolish or stupid actions or expressions on my part? The family had spent many years in building a good reputation and how quickly a member of that family can tear that excellent record down.

I have thought of her words often in the fifty-three years that have passed since those words were spoken. They have helped me keep my nose pointed in the right direction, my actions proper and my speech such that would not mar the family's reputation.

As we move through the world, not only our family's reputation is at stake, but also the reputation of our church and Christianity as a whole. How we live, act and speak announces to the world what influence our religion has on our daily life.

People normally know the faith we are and they judge our religion by the manner in which we conduct ourselves, speak and act. When people review our lives they can observe how important our faith life really is to us. If we speak and act like Christians, people will notice, be influenced, and will be motivated and directed toward our faith.

The eyes of others are always upon us; they watch our every move. They listen to the words that fall from our lips and they are prone to judge rather quickly on how we match up against our great model, Jesus Christ.

We will be celebrating Epiphany [in 1996] on Sunday, January 7. Epiphany comes from a Greek word meaning "manifestation." How well do we manifest the Christ who is our model for every hour, day and week of our lives?

My mother's words could easily be changed a little to: "Please don't ever embarrass the Church, which has your membership." †

Our actions need to match up
to our great model, Jesus Christ.

Let's give thanks for other peoples' good fortune

One of the great green-eyed monsters of life is envy. How terribly it afflicts the hearts and souls of many people; it is not uncommon to see this green monster push its head forward in the lives of many. There are individuals who feel envious of other people's success and achievements, who are unhappy within when someone else has a newer car, a newer house, a newer boat or motor, or a newer "something." They act as if someone else's gain is their loss rather than rejoicing in the good fortune of others, or the accomplishments they have attained, the victories they have won. How often keeping up with the Jones, as the old adage goes, drives people to unbelievable limits to gain this or that. Envy is a terrible spiritual illness — a sin. Consider that every gift, every blessing, comes from God. If God chooses to give another more, wouldn't it seem realistic to praise God for the giving of that gift rather than to be envious of it?

You might wonder what prompted all of this. It actually was what I heard at the State Fair. I can't tell you how many times people came to me in the Dining Hall or out in front, to say how happy they were for us that we had a new diner, that it looked so beautiful and was working out in such splendid fashion. They felt badly for us at the time of the fire but now were rejoicing in our new success. I had so many good feelings every day as this response was repeated time and time again by a multitude of different people of all ages. They were happy we have finished our building, that it is in full operation, that it is brand new, and looks so neat and clean and spacious. They were happy that we were back serving our excellent meals.

How often during these past nine days, I thought, how grand a world it would be if everyone rejoiced over other peoples' good fortune, their success, their achievements, the bounty they may be

The new Epiphany Country Diner.

possessing and enjoying! God has given to each of us everything we have and are. How appropriate and fitting it is that we trust God, and that what He has given to one, and maybe not to another, has been done with infinite wisdom.

I have reaffirmed a powerful lesson over these past nine days. The lesson is: gratitude for other peoples' good fortune.

If someone else enjoys a special good fortune, or blessing, or achievement, be happy for them and tell them so. They will be grateful for your kind words, and appreciative that others are happy when good fortune comes their way.

How little I realized all of the above, when I saw smoke pouring from our Dining Hall a year ago, and that from the smoke, fire and ashes, there would emerge some wonderful experiences from generous hearts. Loyal people have pulled together to make it all happen, bigger and better than ever.

It's a great world we live in, made even better when we rejoice over the success of each other. †

We only walk the pathway of life once

Can you think of a word that changes the whole direction of your life? The word has eight letters, begins with an A and has three Ts and of course it spells ATTITUDE. One adage states, "Attitude is everything." If you want to split hairs, it perhaps isn't everything, but it surely makes a whale of a difference in our whole approach to life. Our attitude affects what we get out of every day and how we approach the activities of that day. How we handle the varying difficulties of daily life is influenced by our attitude.

Dawn Mannella told me about a store in Ridgedale Shopping Center called Successories, which is loaded with all kinds of positive sayings and positive things. I haven't seen it but it certainly sounds very interesting. There is a wonderful saying in the store that reads, "You can't change the wind, but you can adjust your sails."

Many people need a change of attitude more than they need a change of shirt or shoes. Watch the expressions of people as you walk sidewalks, hallways or ride an elevator. You would often think they've never had a good day since the day they were born.

I shall never forget one of my visits to Mercy Hospital some years ago. I saw two ladies who had identical surgeries for their gall bladders. It was absolutely phenomenal how their cases were identical; both were the same age, both had the same doctor, both were operated on the same day, one after the other. On going into the first room I asked the lady how it was going and she said, "Absolutely awful; it was just terrible. My doctor told me it was the worst case he had ever seen and, Father, you can't imagine the pain that I am going through. I'll probably be in here for days to recover."

Her face expressed more pain than her words. I shared a few words of consolation, a blessing and wished her a better day tomorrow.

On going into the next room, I asked the patient, "How's it going?" She said, "No problem. The surgery was a piece of cake;

I'll be out of here before you know it, up-and-at 'em, no problem whatsoever."

It was like going from pitch black night into the brightness and glory of a magnificent sunrise. One word would easily explain the difference in the two rooms — attitude.

The other day, as I was walking the hallway at Mercy Hospital, I met two ladies. I smiled and asked, "How's it going?" The younger of the two smiled and said, "I've never had a better day."

What a glorious response! It dumped a whole gallon of adrenaline into my bloodstream and I was really ready to go for another eight hours.

We only walk this pathway of life once and we may as well brighten it up as best we can. We can either be hanging the dark paper of melancholy or we can be spreading rainbows, moon beams and sun rays wherever we go. The option is always ours. The alternatives are there, they are clear, they are obvious; the choice is ours. Attitude doesn't take away the pain or remove the troubles and the problems, but it surely makes them a lot easier to bear.

We need to teach our little ones to say "excellent." It even changes the expressions on their faces.

Our feet may ache, our back may be sore, a headache may pound in the background and things may not be the brightest at work or in the neighborhood, but if we are walking with God, we know the final outcome and the eternal results. With that awareness and knowledge, our attitude can be excellent!

We can't change the wind but we surely can adjust our sails. †

God has forgiven us; we must do the same

Three of the most beautiful words in the world are: *I forgive you.*

How much more peace there would be in the world if each and every one of us learned the virtue of forgiveness and then practiced it with all our hearts?

Many families are torn apart because individuals refuse to pardon, to put aside the grievances, the mistakes, the troubles of former years. They harden their hearts and insist it be their way or no way. When the opportunity presents itself they pick open the sores of former days.

Some years ago when fire gutted our State Fair Dining Hall and it was no longer usable, something new had to be built. Herbst and Sons graciously came and leveled the building for us. They hauled away all of the debris and left the ground clean and unlittered. We then began to build a new Dining Hall, which has served us so beautifully ever since. We could have stood and rung our hands looking at the scarred and burnt remains of the building and bemoaned the unfortunate happening. This would have accomplished nothing. We could still be standing there, but we needed to put the fire behind us and move on. So also it is with arguments, quarrels, disagreements and discontent. We need to forgive, put them aside, bury them in a pit, cover them over and begin anew. It you have grievances and unforgiven realities in your life, why not forgive or pardon and move on with a new beginning? It's very refreshing.

The great purpose of the Son of God coming to earth was to forgive us, redeem us and bring us back to the Father's household. How beautifully God forgives our sins, puts them aside and says to us merely: *Go and sin no more.*

On Mercy Sunday we rejoice and bask in the great mercy of God, thanking our God for His tremendous spirit of forgiveness to us. Where would we be at if God never forgave us? We would be buried in the depths of Hell.

God has forgiven us so generously; we must do the same with all people. We often repeat the verse: *Have mercy on us, oh God.*

Have mercy on us. Wouldn't it be wonderful if we turned and had mercy on all of those who had annoyed, irritated, troubled or bothered us in any way? Start today to forgive and forget; put the wrong doings of yesterday behind you, and greet each day with a new and magnificent beginning. ✝

There are great payoffs
in the game called life

How would you feel if you won the Big Lotto, being a winner of maybe $15 million or $20 million with a fabulous payoff of hundreds of thousands of dollars a year? Instead of worrying about how to pay the bills, you would rather be worrying about how to spend the money. And, I am sure it would not be without lots of trials and tribulations because everyone and their brother-in-law would be knocking at your door for a handout. Your peace and quiet would soon be a forgotten ingredient of life unless you moved away to where no one knew you and surely even then the word would get out that you had lots and lots of money to spend. The time would come, I am sure, when you would maybe appreciate just being one of the poor people moving around through life unknown to anyone else.

Nothing is really free and a price needs to be paid for just about everything we happen to come across in life. The time would perhaps come when you would just maybe prefer having that little old rocking chair in front of some humble little cottage in the sunny south.

The biggest Lotto ever played is the one that God Himself runs and the beauty of it is that everyone can win. There need be no losers. All God asks is that we play the game day-by-day and that we invest the wonderful little things that can fill each day: the little expressions of kindness and thoughtfulness to this person or that one, a pinch of patience and self-discipline, some compassion and understanding to lift up, encourage, and support those whose legs are crumbling a bit.

There are great payoffs in the game called life. The Lord directs the game and sets up the rules for playing. They come under two great umbrellas, one which reads: *Love your God with your whole heart*, and the other, *Love your neighbor as yourself*. The payoff is the Great Kingdom of the Father, called Heaven, where joys are eternal and the fulfillment is beyond our wildest expectations.

When we will win this prize no one knows. It could be today, tomorrow or the next day. It could be in five years, twenty-five years, fifty-five years or ninety-five years.

Whenever you see advertisements or hear talk about Lotto Minnesota or any of the Lottos, perhaps it could be a little reminder of the big Lotto that God plays with us day-by-day. It's a reality that we could well remind ourselves of as we go through the pathways of this earth's experience. Everyone can win. All we need do is follow the rules of the game. †

Cure for apathy is getting involved

If you took your car and parked it out in the field, whether it is new, or a few years old, and just left it sit there, what would happen? Before long it wouldn't be worth a great deal, because the lack of operation and activity would slowly destroy it. The elements of nature would take their toll and soon the parts would not function. We don't just park it and leave it sit.

The United Way had a marvelous ad that read: *The three biggest killers in America today are cancer, heart disease and apathy.*

The first two are readily recognizable, but the third, apathy, is one we perhaps do not think about very frequently as so destructive. When you ponder over cases of apathy, the truth becomes more obvious with each passing reflection.

Apathy is parking ourselves and becoming oblivious of all others.

Apathy is a destructive force, whether in a child, a teenager or a senior citizen. The "I don't care" attitude slowly destroys the vigor, vim and vitality of the person. It surrounds itself with indifference, isolation, moodiness and often despondency. A lack of self-esteem sets in and before long even the outward appearance of the individual begins to go downhill. The person builds a very secure wall around self and defies any attempt for communication or developing a relationship. Apathy, like crabgrass, works its way into the various areas of the person.

What's the cure for apathy? Two words would be a good starter: GET INVOLVED.

Yes, discover some area where you can share some of yourself, your time and talents. Your presence can be a wonderful gift to many. Move out into the world around you and share yourself. Make the day of others better by your very presence. Go to a nursing home with a book or a magazine and read to someone who needs a little time to be occupied. Have a deck of cards in your pocket to share a few hours with someone else. There are some wonderful seniors who would love a ride out in the country. If you have a few hours to kill why not call up some young mother who has a few little ones and go over and watch her kids. Tell her to "take a powder" for a few hours, to window-shop or just get away. If you're a teen and are bored, why not roll up your sleeves and clean the garage or the basement, or do some odd jobs for a senior who needs a helping hand or anyone who needs your youthful endeavor? Do it without pay; the reward is greater.

Tracy Sigfrid gave me the ad from the United Way and pinned a little note with it: *You can help cure apathy by caring. Please give generously whether it's by volunteering your time to the church, giving an extra dollar, or helping your neighbor or another parishioner in our Christian family. Let's all cure apathy by caring a little more.*

When we get out of the little world of self and explore the wonderful world of others, it is then that we find excitement, joy, peace, happiness, and fulfillment in our lives. †

Our Heavenly Father
knows all that we need

When will it be? Is it coming soon? How should I prepare? Those are commonly asked questions concerning the end of the world.

With the New Millennium [2000] coming soon, there is growing concern that the end is not far distant. The above questions grace my ears many times a month. I thought it might be appropriate to share my Ramblings on the subject. The thoughts I will share are entirely mine and not the reflections of others. I will share some Biblical quotes in support of my observations.

In nearly fifty years of priestly ministry, I have survived at least seven predicted ends of the world. I would be informed it was coming on a particular date in an upcoming year. Thankfully all failed to materialize, which is quite obvious.

I have had a good number of suggestions to store food, clothing, candles and other items for the days ahead, advised that these will be critical for survival during the days of trial and affliction. These have created great concern and apprehension for many of the faithful. In 2,000 years of Christianity, the followers of Christ have suffered some terrible afflictions, but Jesus has always been there to support them. The persecutions by the Roman Emperors were brutal, ruthless and covered the period from Christ to the Edict of Constantine in 313 A.D., a period of 280 years. The more the Romans persecuted, the more the Christians flourished.

For those who tell me to store things up for days of trial ahead, I recall the words of Jesus to His Disciples as He sent them forth: *He instructed them to take nothing for the journey but a walking stick — no food, no sack, no money in their belts. They were, however, to wear sandals but not a second tunic.* (Mark 6:8-9)

One of my favorite Scripture passages is: *Do not live in fear, little flock. It has pleased your Father to give you the Kingdom.* (Luke 12:32)

What beautiful imagery; Jesus like a mother hen, watching over His little chicks, His children. How vividly I can recall on the farm the mother hen in time of danger, collecting all the chicks under her spread-out wings.

Our Lord wasn't given to worrying: *Stop worrying, then, over questions like, 'What are we to eat, or what are we to drink, or what are we to wear?' The unbelievers are always running after these things. Your heavenly Father knows all that you need. Seek first His kingship over you, His way of holiness, and all these things will be given you besides. Enough, then, of worrying about tomorrow. Let tomorrow take care of itself. Today has troubles enough of its own.* (Matthew 6:31-34)

One of the great Scripture verses is: *The Kingdom of Heaven is at hand.* (Matthew 4:17)

Yesterday is gone forever — I always call it a dead horse; tomorrow I cannot live today, so my only concern is to give today my very best effort for the Lord. It is in the present moment that I work out my salvation. St. Peter said in his Epistle: *Fear not and do not stand in awe of what this people fears.* (1 Peter 3:14)

In summary: I don't know when the end is coming, soon or later, but my preparation is focused on today, to live it as if it were my last day and leave the rest to God. Keep smiling; fear not. God, like the mother hen, is watching closely. ✝

Live in the present
to the best of your ability

I have many people asking questions like, "Is the world going to end on New Year's Day 2000?" or "Is it all going to shut down during the year 2000? Is it true that the end of the world is imminent and will happen any moment now?"

The answer to those questions was given by Jesus Christ 2,000 years ago. He said: *As for the exact day or hour, no one knows it, neither the angels in Heaven nor the Son, but the Father only.* (Matthew 24:36)

In His human nature, Jesus was stating that this was a time known only by God Himself.

A careful reading of the four Gospels certainly reminds us that our Lord is telling us continually to live the present day. He said: *The reign of God is at hand.* (Luke 10:9) This means that the moment of salvation is right now.

What are we doing with this present moment to praise our God and prepare for the next world? In the last two weeks we have had eleven deaths in our parish. For those people, the end of the world was at the moment of death. They are not concerned about whether it is going to happen on this or that particular date in the year 2000. It was all over for them the moment their souls left their bodies.

To the many inquiries concerning when the end of the world is coming, the best response is: live this present moment, this present day to the best of your ability, striving to please God and follow His ways.

So many are continually worrying about when the end of the world is going to come. The end for each of us is when we die, and our death is an unknown reality—it may be today, tomorrow or next month, or ten years down the road. Since I don't know when the end is coming, it is best I live today as if it were my last.

The following was given to me by Tom Raiche. It has some marvelous thoughts for each person. Read it attentively and prayerfully.

To realize the value of one year:
Ask a student who has failed a final exam.
To realize the value of one month:
Ask a mother who has given birth to a premature baby.
To realize the value of one week:
Ask an editor of a weekly newspaper.
To realize the value of one hour:
Ask the lovers who are waiting to meet.
To realize the value of one minute:
Ask a person who has missed the train, bus or plane.
To realize the value of one second:
Ask a person who has survived an accident.
To realize the value of one millisecond:
Ask the person who has won a silver medal in the Olympics.

Time waits for no one. Treasure every moment you have. You will treasure it even more when you can share it with someone special. †

God doesn't send us to Hell; we send ourselves

Some years ago, I was giving a young fellow pre-marriage instructions. In those days, we were required to give six instructions on the Catholic Faith. My first two classes didn't make much of a dent upon him and he showed practically zero enthusiasm; his outward physical posture surely confirmed that fact. I thought perhaps I might awaken him a bit, so I decided the next class to give him a one-hour session on Hell. I quoted every possible relevant Scriptural passage to him, and used, very extensively, the section on Hell in Dante's Divine Comedy. I quoted some of the great Saints, and after an hour of this information, he looked up and said, "Is this all really true?"

I responded, "If you can trust the words of the Son of God, namely Jesus Christ, then it demands some very attentive consideration."

He left visibly disturbed and when he came back the following week he looked at me and said, "If everything you said last week is really true, and I believe it is, then here is one man who really needs to change his life."

This he did in magnificent fashion. He finished the course of instructions, became a Catholic and thereafter never missed Sunday Mass or the reception of Holy Communion. He came to Confession with great regularity and this person who was once a loose-living individual became a tower of spiritual strength. That which disturbed the young man the most was the eternal nature of the sufferings of Hell, whatever they may be. He realized that in Hell there is no hope, never a better day, nothing to anticipate, just one continuous, endless stream of suffering and pain.

The one element that always sustains people, gives them encouragement is the virtue of hope. In the longest of days and darkest of nights, if there is a shred or even a little shaft of hope, there is encouragement to the individual. What must be the devastation when you live in the complete absence of that hope!

The Bible refers to the worm that never dies, meaning the worm of regret, remorse, that something could have all been so very different had we not placed ourselves in a dreadful situation. God sends no one to Hell; we send ourselves by our free choices, our deliberate actions, our determination to do it our way rather than God's way.

In the Gospel of Matthew it is written that Our Lord at the Final Judgment of the world will address the dammed by saying: *Out of My sight, you condemned, into that everlasting fire prepared for the devil and his angels!* (Matthew 25:41)

This is a sentence that can never be contested, revoked or appealed. The determination to do it our way has terrible consequences.

These thoughts were prompted last Friday afternoon as I was out making Holy Communion calls to the sick. It was a day when everyone was speaking of the heat. Can you imagine having every day be hot like last Friday, and many times worse, with no air conditioning, no movement of wind, no breeze, just the stark reality of 100 degrees Fahrenheit, or more?

If you haven't been walking with the Lord, don't put off joining hands with Him another day. You know neither the day nor the hour when God will call. Another day may be too late. Seize upon the opportunity, the "here and now," that God lays before you.

Spiritual realities are so easy to ignore and pass by. It is incumbent upon all of us to face reality, to encounter the truth and to discern where we really are at in our relationship with God.

The many jokes about Hell make very light of its terrible reality. It is vital to face the truth about Hell head on and know that it is a possibility for anyone unless they walk with the Lord Jesus and follow His teachings. ✝

Something better is coming!

There was a woman who had been diagnosed with cancer and had been given three months to live. Her doctor told her to start making preparations to die (something we all should be doing all of the time), so she contacted her pastor and had him come to her house to discuss certain aspects of her final wishes. She told him which songs she wanted sung at the service, what Scripture passages she would like read, and what she wanted to be wearing. The woman also told her pastor that she wanted to be buried with her favorite Bible.

Everything was in order and the pastor was preparing to leave when the woman suddenly remembered something very important to her. "There's one more thing," she said excitedly.

"What's that?" came the pastor's reply.

"This is very important," the woman continued. "I want to be buried with a fork in my right hand."

The pastor stood looking at the woman not knowing quite what to say.

"That shocks you, doesn't it?" the woman asked.

"Well, to be honest, I'm puzzled by the request," said the pastor.

The woman explained. "In all my years of attending church socials and functions where food was involved, my favorite part was when whoever was clearing away the dishes of the main course would lean over and say, "You can keep your fork." It was my favorite part because I knew something better was coming. When they told me to keep my fork, I knew that something great was about to be given to me. It wasn't Jell-O or pudding but cake or pie, something with substance. So I just want people to see me there in that casket with a fork in my hand and I want them to wonder, "What's with the fork?" Then I want you to tell them, "Something better is coming, so keep your fork, too."

The pastor's eyes welled up with tears of joy as he hugged the woman goodbye. He knew this would be one of the last times he would see her before her death. But he also knew that this woman had a better grasp of Heaven than he did. She KNEW that something better was coming.

At the funeral people were walking by the woman's casket, they saw the pretty dress she was wearing, her favorite Bible, and the fork placed in her right hand. Over and over the pastor heard the question, "What's with the fork?" and over and over he smiled.

During his short message, the pastor told the people of the conversation he had with the woman shortly before she died. He also told them about the fork and what it symbolized to her. The pastor told the people how he could not stop thinking about the fork and told them that they probably would not be able to stop thinking about it either. He was right.

So the next time you reach down for your fork, let it remind you, oh so gently, that there is something better coming! †

Approach the end with a deep faith

Some years ago it was always an embarrassing moment for a lady to have someone come up and whisper quietly in her ear, "Your slip is showing." There would be a mad dash to the nearest restroom and the embarrassing situation would be corrected. Knowing our present generation with slacks and shorts, those moments of sensitivity happen very infrequently.

Now that I have your attention, I would like to move on to another line, mainly, your faith is showing! This past week we had six funerals; they ranged in age from infant to elderly. Losing a loved one is always a very, very difficult time and certainly much emotion is displayed, and rightly so, for it is good to get the feelings out and to release the pent up sorrow within.

People cope with death in a great variety of ways, but certainly one of the finest means and methods of approaching death is with a deep faith, an awareness of God and His master plan for all of us. For Almighty God, death is a natural consequence of being born. We need to be born into this world to be alive and we need to die to be born into eternity.

For the believer, death is just another chapter in that great experience of an individual's life. Our stay on planet Earth can be short or very long but all lengths are very short in comparison to our stay in eternity, which will never end.

Since Epiphany began, [until the time of this column] there have been 2,234 deaths in the parish. They have been at all ages of life, from birth to 100 years of age. One reality continually surfaces and it is very visible and evident, that is, the degree of coping, of bearing the burden of death, is in a great proportion to the degree of faith and the belief in God that rests in the souls of the survivors.

Faith is that marvelous ingredient within the soul, which places things in their proper order and arrangement. The death is not seen only as an event in time, but mostly in the reality of eternity. The material, the transitory, are shifted to the sidelines and we move into the sphere of the eternal, that marvelous reality of eternity of which St. Paul said: *Eye has not seen, ear has not heard, nor has it so much as dawned on man what God has prepared for those who love Him.* (1 Corinthians 2:9)

The wise virgins spoken of in Matthew's Gospel, Chapter 25, are those people who go through the process of daily life, filling their jars always with the oil of the spirit, the oil of prayer and worship, the oil of kindness and goodness, the oil of patience and generosity, the oil of living the Christ life in our daily lives, and bringing Christ to the world in which we move and live and act.

Death comes to every family, eventually, and when it does come, the faith within our life will be a powerful force to sustain you. It will be self evident; it will be a stabling factor amidst your tears. It will be a guiding light through your sorrowing moment. It will give you hope when things seem so dark and despairing. It will give you assurance that death is not an end, but a new wonderful beginning on the shores of eternity, where those family and friends who have preceded you in death will be there with open hearts to greet you and welcome you in. So as you leave one group of friends and relatives on Earth, there will be whole legions of them in eternity to welcome you into the next.

Yes, my prayer is that your faith will be showing when death comes to your home. †

Our purpose on Earth
is to leave and join God in Heaven

Death is something that each and every one of us will encounter. Much is written about it and it is a word that brings anxiety and certainly a great measure of trepidation to great numbers of people. Death means the separation of loved ones, that we shall no longer see them on this earth, that our lifestyle will be changed. Death is the great moment which puts aside all of the things of this earth, and then, only the realities of the next life are meaningful.

The Bible has much to say about death, dying, and about future life. The real great purpose of our existence and of being born is to eventually leave this earth and live with God in Heaven.

I've seen many, many leave this earth in my years of priesthood, and each time I watch another go, I say to myself, "Now they know what it is all about. Now they see reality and truth in all of its magnificent beauty and glory. Now they have the real perspective and dimension of human existence."

There are many things written about death and dying and one of those items was sent to me a few weeks ago by a friend. It gives such a marvelous perception of what death is all about that I'd like to share it with you:

I am standing by the seashore. A ship at my side spreads her white sails to the morning breeze and starts for the blue ocean. She is an object of beauty and strength. And I stand and watch her until at length she is only a ribbon of white cloud just where the sea and sky come to mingle with each other. Then someone at my side says, 'There, she's gone!!!'

Gone where? Gone from my sight, that's all. She is just as large in mast and hull and spar as she was when she left my side, and just as able to bear her load of living freight to her place of destination. Her diminished size is in me, not in her, and just at the moment when someone at my side says, 'There, she's gone,' there are other eyes watching her coming and other voices ready to take up the glad shout, 'Here she comes!'

And that is dying...

Yes, on the other side, all of those relatives and friends, the people who knew the individual here on earth, are standing on the shores of the Heavenly Kingdom, seeing the individual coming to them, and what a great shout they must indeed raise when one of their loved ones joins their great company of Saints in the Kingdom.

P.S. The next time you are sharing a death with someone who has lost a loved one, perhaps the above couple of paragraphs might be a great source of comfort and help to them. †

We all need 'eternal' vision

Don't sweat the little things. It is an old saying we often hear, and how true it is as we walk the path of life. How many arguments, quarrels, and explosions are over little things that really don't amount to much more than a row of peppers in the field? As we look back over disagreements and other contentions, we frequently reflect: and to think that I got so hot and bothered over something as small and meaningless as that!

We all need to have a good vision of life and see daily happenings in relationship to eternal life. I often ask myself (and others), "How important will this be when I come to die? How meaningful will it be in eternity?" That establishes a good balance and gives one the opportunity of really assessing the value of the situation at hand. If we take all things in the light of eternity, it's much easier to come to conclusions and decisions, to determine how much effort or energy this or that should demand of us, whether we should become concerned but certainly not upset!

We all have one great goal in life and that is to gain Heaven. If we accomplish that, we have done very, very well. It is good to put that reality on one side of the balance scale and then put our concerns and worries and apprehensions on the other.

We often talk about 20/20 vision as the vision we all wish to maintain. We all need another form of vision, though, something better than 20/20 vision, and that is eternal vision — the vision of evaluating all things in the light of salvation or gaining the Kingdom of Heaven.

How often family peace is disturbed or ruined by little things, such as somebody spilling the proverbial glass of milk, burning the supper, or tracking some dirt on the freshly vacuumed carpet. We don't do these things deliberately to annoy someone, but if they are indeed accidents, let's treat them as such and move on with life.

Hear both sides before you jump prematurely to any conclusions, and when the facts are all on the table in good order, it is a lot easier to conclude what to do, say or think.

In the Gospel, Jesus says: *Look at the birds in the sky. They do not sow or reap, they gather nothing into barns; yet your heavenly Father feeds them. Are not you more important than they?* (Matthew 6:26)

God will do no less for each of us.

Don't let the little things, or even the big things, get under your skin. They are like the little pebbles in the bottom of your shoe that really cause a lot of irritation, or the speck in your eye or the bit of dirt on your glasses. Remove them quietly and move on with life. Don't let them disturb your tranquility, your peace or your harmony in life. Life is too short to miss making every day a wonderful experience, a day filled with joy, happiness and peace.

A theme to remember: "Don't sweat the little things." Consider its effect on eternity; if it is meaningless, don't worry and move on. †

Commit yourself to Heaven being your ultimate goal

If someone asked you what is your long term goal, how would you respond? Depending on your age, the response may be quite different. A student would perhaps say to gain a college degree. Those just out of college might say to get a good long-term job. Others, later on in their years, may be speaking of an early retirement or some other worldly achievement.

One of our dear senior citizens was asked that question when she was at the age of ninety. Her response was quick, to the point and certainly inspiring. She said very shortly, "Heaven, of course."

What a magnificent response to a challenging question! And those last two words, "of course," indicate that it was an understood reality. Nothing else could take the place of her long-term goal. Heaven was an accepted reality of her life and, that being true, all things would surely be directed to that particular end.

Louise Haben was ninety when she made the above response. She continued to live until she was ninety-three years of age. (She passed away March 5, 1992.)

What a beautiful reality to have the goal and purpose of life so clearly in mind, to know exactly why you are here and where you are going. To know where life should end and where we are going would certainly assist us in making the right decisions, the proper moves, to know exactly what is important and what is of little importance in the various choices and decisions we make.

If we knew and really were committed to the reality that Heaven is our great goal, then every decision must be made with that particular objective in mind. Will this or that particular action, or this particular deal or venture of business lead me closer to gaining my eventual goal or will it turn me away? Will this particular relationship be of profit to me in gaining that great Kingdom or will it make its attainment less likely and far more difficult?

God made us to be happy with Him someday in the next, and therefore all things must head in that direction, if they are to be for our advantage and well being.

Racing around this good earth of ours will be advantageous only if it leads us to the right goal — the Kingdom of Heaven. Keep your sights on that, and decisions will be quite easily made, for we need only ask, "Will it help me attain my end or lead me away from it?"

Louise had a good life, was dedicated to her God and to her family. She was well prepared when the bell rang for her to go to the next life. She had spent many wonderful years in preparing for that grand entry and that preparation was certainly in harmony and response to knowing where she was going.

And so when you are asked the great question, what is your long-term goal? Louise's response might well be recalled: "Heaven, of course." †

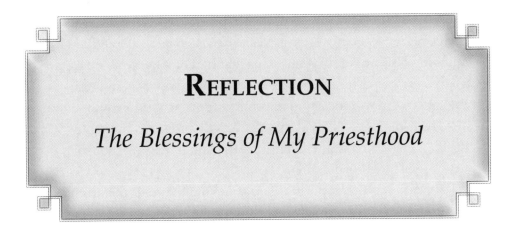

REFLECTION

The Blessings of My Priesthood

THE BLESSINGS OF MY PRIESTHOOD

My years of priesthood have been a wonderful and exciting experience. Working for the Lord has many great benefits beyond number. The rewards are eternal and the daily satisfactions are beyond expression.

One of the greatest blessings for me has been job satisfaction, for there has never been a day, in what is now six decades, when I have regretted being a priest. I can scarcely comprehend doing anything else. Some surveys tell us that half of American workers go to their jobs disliking what they do. What a burden and trial that must be day after day. The reality seems beyond imagination.

The experiences in priesthood are as divergent as humanity itself. There is a constant connection to people who are indeed God's finest earthly creation.

A priest has the opportunity to share in the broad spectrum of human emotions from the greatest joys to the deepest sorrows. We share in a couple's experience of a new child and then bask in the spiritual wonderment of the Baptism as the child becomes a member of God's family. We share in the inspirational moments of the First Holy Communion, so filled with devotion and spiritual fervor, a time when grandparents play a marvelous role, with parents, to bring a child to the Lord Jesus. Sharing of the Holy Spirit at Confirmation is always a revitalizing and apostolic time. Happiness prevails in those glorious moments of witnessing the marriage of two people prepared to commit themselves to each other for their entire lives. The moments of joy that a priest can participate in and share are endless.

There are also times of sorrow when grief, trial and tribulation strike a family. What a great opportunity to help relieve the burden and lighten the sorrow that penetrates peoples' hearts and souls. Ministering to the sick also is a very rewarding experience, helping people confront the reality of Calvary in their own lives.

The opportunities for counseling are numerous and satisfying; to see troubled situations made peaceful and strained relationships made comfortable and joyous are gratifying.

Above and beyond all this, however, there are two times that release great joy and happiness. One is the opportunity to forgive sin, to lift the heavy burden of guilt from the souls of people repenting before their all-merciful God. The other — and the greatest joy of all, the pearl of the great price — is to go to the Altar of the Lord and renew Calvary in an unbloody manner, to give the gift of Jesus the Son to the Father, and then to be the recipient of that same gift through Holy Communion. Human and divine are united in a marvelous and wonderful togetherness.

The priesthood has been very good to me and has blessed me beyond expression. I'm grateful to God for every moment He has given me in His service and I shall be delighted to receive as many more as He deems fit to send. †

About Reiser Relief Inc.

Reiser Relief Inc. is a volunteer run non-profit 501(c)(3) corporation founded by Father Bernard Reiser, who has been involved with Haiti outreach programs since 1996. Reiser Relief is based in Coon Rapids, Minnesota, and its mission is to help the impoverished people of Haiti, the poorest country in the Western Hemisphere. The social and environmental problems are the greatest challenges the people of Haiti are facing today.

In the midst of these problems, we are compelled to provide the essential services to aid in day-to-day survival. The services we provide include: fresh water delivery, food centers, housing, primary grade education and eldercare facilities. Many projects are in or near Cité Soleil, the suburb of the Haitian capital of Port au Prince.

One of our original programs that we sponsored was the Village of Jesus, located in the mountain area of Leoganes. There we built a center caring for abandoned women who had no place to live. It currently has dormitories, laundry facilities, kitchen, dining and bathrooms to accommodate these women.

Our school programs provide hope for a better future that comes with an education. Children receive a daily meal at school and for many, this is their only meal for the day. We engage in building and supporting school classrooms and sanitary blocks for sewage. Donations provide for so much — salaries for teachers, text books, food, uniforms and hope. Reiser Relief supports two primary schools: Terre Promise and Reiser Heights Primary.

We assisted in building and supporting medical community centers and sanitary blocks for sewage. We also support clinics and small hospitals in Cité Soleil. The number one cause for illness is the lack of clean water and our water delivery program brings life-saving water daily to those in need. Fresh water is obtained from deep wells and trucked to the areas of need.

The water truck operates six days a week making four deliveries to many neighborhoods in Cité Soleil and reaching numerous impoverished families where the local people carry the water home in five-gallon buckets. With your help, we can affect thousands of lives; without the water we supply to these impoverished people, they cannot survive.

With the Grace of our living God and help of donors, in 2008 Reiser Relief partnered with Healing Haiti, a non-profit organization; together we purchased sixteen acres of land to build Grace Village. It will be a little city of peace including Maranatha Orphanage for handicapped, deaf, orphaned and abandoned children living in severe poverty. A separate facility will be constructed to provide for the elderly. We are pleased to share that in 2009 the ground breaking had begun for Grace Village.

In January 2010, Haiti was hit by a magnitude 7.0 earthquake. Reiser Relief was quick to respond. The day after the earthquake, Reiser Relief, Inc., sent $10,000 for water fuel truck expenses and food purchases. Weeks later, it donated another $10,000 to Feed My Starving Children for ingredients to make MannaPack-Potato nutrition packets, used to treat children suffering from diarrhea, and another $6,000 to offset shipping costs for a cargo food container. It donated another $20,000 for reconstruction of Terra Promise Primary School.

Reiser Relief is committed to providing essential services to aid in day-to-day survival of thousands. We live among abundance; the Haitians live in extreme poverty.

The people of Haiti await your generous response and pray for God's abundant blessings upon you. Visit the Reiser Relief website to learn more about how you can help the effort in Haiti and please donate.

www.ReiserRelief.org

Haiti Prayer

Almighty Father in Heaven, surround the
people of Haiti with Thy Divine Providence.
Strengthen them in their trials,
provide for their needs.

May they join their sufferings to those
of Jesus, God's Son, as they walk through
the rubble of the January earthquake.
May they realize that they are accompanying
Jesus on the road to crucifixion.

May the Joys of Easter unfold in their hearts,
and encourage them to persevere
to Heaven's kingdom.

Amen.

Father Bernard Reiser
April 27, 2010

*He will wipe away all tears from their eyes; there will be no
more death, no more mourning or sadness. The world of the past
has gone.* (Revelation 21:4)